AF576537

Willem de Looper
A Retrospective
Exhibition 1966–1996

willem

A RETROSPECTIVE
EXHIBITION 1966–1996

de looper

Terry Gips,
Curator/Catalogue Editor

Introduction

"Jefferson Place," for most people involved in the arts in Washington, D.C. in the mid 1990s, is simply the name of one of the quieter streets in the Dupont Circle area of the nation's capital. In 1966, however, it referred to gallery at the center of what was new and exciting in the city's art. Named for this quiet street, the Jefferson Place Gallery had, since its inception in 1957, been anything but quiet. For two decades, it fostered some of the most important art produced in the region, and perhaps the only art to put Washington on the map as the source of a significant movement—the Washington Color School. It was as well the locus for Willem de Looper's first solo exhibition, a critical marker in the enormously productive thirty years chronicled by this retrospective.

As Howard Risatti makes clear in his catalogue essay, Willem de Looper has long been associated with—if not the key figure in—the second phase of the Washington Color School, extending its life and enriching its meaning. De Looper's oeuvre, however, should not be confined to this association or to simple conceptions of colorfield painting or geometric abstraction. As evidenced by this exhibition, de Looper has pushed the possibilities of paint and surface, color and form, in continually inventive ways, bringing freshness to this genre long after others had abandoned it for other agendas. His work confirms color and abstraction as enduring forces in our aesthetic vocabulary.

Willem de Looper has poured, rolled, sprayed, brushed, and daubed rich acrylic pigments on canvas, board, and paper for well over thirty years, amassing an immense body of work. Much of this work has been seen in galleries and museums in Washington and elsewhere around the country. However, most of the exhibitions have featured works from a limited period of time and have not included enough works to provide a comprehensive view of Willem de Looper as an artist. This exhibition at The Art Gallery at the University of Maryland attempts to remedy this situation by presenting a substantial collection of exemplary works that trace de Looper's progression from 1966 to 1996.

The Art Gallery recently identified as a critical part of its mission the presentation of retrospective exhibitions for mid-career artists who have played principal roles in the cultural life of the region. Willem de Looper's name immediately arose for this series. In many ways, no other artist so epitomizes the making of art in the Washington region. Not only has his work been highly visible in the city throughout the last three decades, but de Looper's position as former curator at the Phillips Collection also put him mid-stream in the cultural life of Washington.

When I approached de Looper about this exhibition, he expressed enthusiasm and came to visit us in College Park. Impressed that our space could accommodate some of his very large canvases as well as a sizable number of the mid-size and smaller works, he quickly became a partner in what has been a truly collaborative adventure. From the first visits to his home and studio to see paintings and slides and to talk about his work, through all the many subsequent visits, faxes, and phone calls, the process of working with Willem has been enriching and exciting.

Howard Risatti, who has closely followed de Looper's work over the years, joined the project early on and helped shape the selection of works as he developed the catalogue essay. Much later, graphic designer John Lavery became an important player as catalogue designer, and helped conceptualize the printed documentation of our undertaking.

Certainly there were anxieties along the way—tracking down missing slides, confirming and reconfirming dates and dimensions of works, revising the catalogue chronology again and again, learning that keys to his storage space were missing after transporting paintings to College Park, and so on. But throughout it all, Willem was patient and good-humored. There was always coffee to drink, and Frauke, Willem's wife, often would go out and bring back sandwiches from a nearby deli providing sustenance which enabled us to continue working.

And best of all were the wonderful conversations with an artist who has lived, loved, and breathed art for most of his life. Willem always seems to have some new story about art and artists in Washington; the museums and the curators; the patrons and the critics. From him I learned an enormous amount about the history of Washington art in the second half of the twentieth century—a fascinating story waiting to be told. The chronology which follows Risatti's essay was conceptualized, first of all, to chronicle the evolution of Willem de Looper's life and career. But as this section developed, it became clear that it would be greatly enhanced by paralleling de Looper's chronology with the events which influenced his life and work, especially the unfolding events of the Washington art scene.

This history of Washington art from the fifties to the present makes no pretense at being the ultimate word on the subject, time limitations making impossible the total corroboration of facts, dates, and names. It is simply an initial inquiry, one chapter in a book waiting to be written. We regret any errors, oversights, and omissions that inevitably come with a massive undertaking of this nature. However, we concluded that, even with its shortcomings, this information about Washington would be essential to anyone interested in the life and work of Willem de Looper, and might, in fact, inspire further documentation and scholarship on this important era in the culture of the capital.

As this catalogue goes to press and we approach the installation date, Willem de Looper is at home in his studio creating yet another body of paintings and working on yet another of his delightful and enigmatic sketchbooks. He had just made a trip to Arizona and New Mexico in June, and knowing this gave me a better sense of his instinctive use of new and residual experience. In particular, I noted how de Looper, like so many American artists before him, relishes the expansive spaces and simple forms of the Southwest landscape. In this, I again saw the artist's affinities with early American modernists, and particularly with Dove whose work continues to be a direct inspiration. While many of his paintings appear to draw much of their energy from the urban and cerebral environment of the east, I was struck by the subtle calming impact seemingly introduced by elements of the Southwest into the formal structures of his paintings. Throughout all the chaos brought on by preparing this exhibition and catalogue, what seemed to remain foremost for Willem was continuing to work. It is with great respect that I note this. Curating this exhibition and witnessing Willem de Looper's passion to paint has a been a pleasure and a privilege.

Terry Gips, *Curator*
August, 1996

Acknowledgements

There were many without whom this thirty-year retrospective exhibition and catalogue of the work of Willem de Looper would not have happened. First, I wish to recognize and thank the many donors who made this project possible. They are listed at the end of the catalogue. Helen Frederick's involvement in the production of the commemorative prints at Pyramid Atlantic was also an essential part of the early fundraising process. Next, I would like to thank the private collectors, The Corcoran Gallery of Art, the Hirshhorn Museum and Sculpture Garden, and The Phillips Collection who generously loaned paintings, thus enabling us to include some of the artist's most significant works.

One person who was not only instrumental in the early stages of this project, but continued to provide encouragement throughout was Sally Troyer. In fact, it was at the Troyer Fitzpatrick Lassman Gallery that I first became acquainted with de Looper's work in the eighties. Troyer's partners, Sandra Fitzpatrick and Vivienne Lassman, also provided their enthusiastic help. I wish also to thank Sally for her short catalogue essay on de Looper's sketchbooks. Statements contributed by other colleagues of the artist, Laughlin Phillips, Wilfred Brunner, Manfred Baumgartner, and Lenore Miller, also added greatly to our appreciation of de Looper's work.

Of course, Howard Risatti's essay is central to the catalogue. I am very grateful for all of the work he put into this text, and I acknowledge the impact our conversations had on my own understanding of de Looper's work. I also wish to thank the Gallery's 1995-96 graduate assistant, Mary Jo Aagerstoun for her primary research on the chronology of Willem de Looper's life and for the contextualizing history of American art, especially that being produced in Washington from 1950 to the present. She conducted several interviews with de Looper and sifted through numerous notebooks and boxes of exhibition announcements and reviews, correspondence, slides, and family photographs. From this she drafted the two parallel narratives. Cara McCormack, an undergraduate student who worked throughout the summer, deserves considerable praise for her contributions to every aspect of the project, from the endless organizational office tasks to numerous physical jobs which were critical in realizing the catalogue and exhibition.

For the elegance of the finished catalogue I thank, first, John Lavery who designed it and insisted on aiming for the very best, and even a bit more. Second, I thank the superb team from Virginia Lithograph, especially Beth Kent and Mitch Rockwell, who were extraordinarily generous with their time and exceptional skills as well as relaxed and collaborative in their work with John and myself. It is indeed sad that Beth did not live to see this project reach fruition. Another essential player in the catalogue was Greg Staley who completed the challenging task of photographing the paintings.

I also express my gratitude to the staff of the Gallery for their hard work on many aspects of the project, and to the College of Arts and Humanities at the University of Maryland which has supported this exhibition and The Art Gallery as a whole.

I thank Frauke de Looper for her enthusiasm and patience, and for her editorial assistance on the chronology.

Finally, I thank Willem de Looper for his unending work on the exhibition and catalogue and most importantly, for the art he has created and continues to create.

T. Gips

Untitled, 1975
48" x 48"
acrylic on canvas
Collection of Mr. and Mrs. Freidenrich
Figure 1

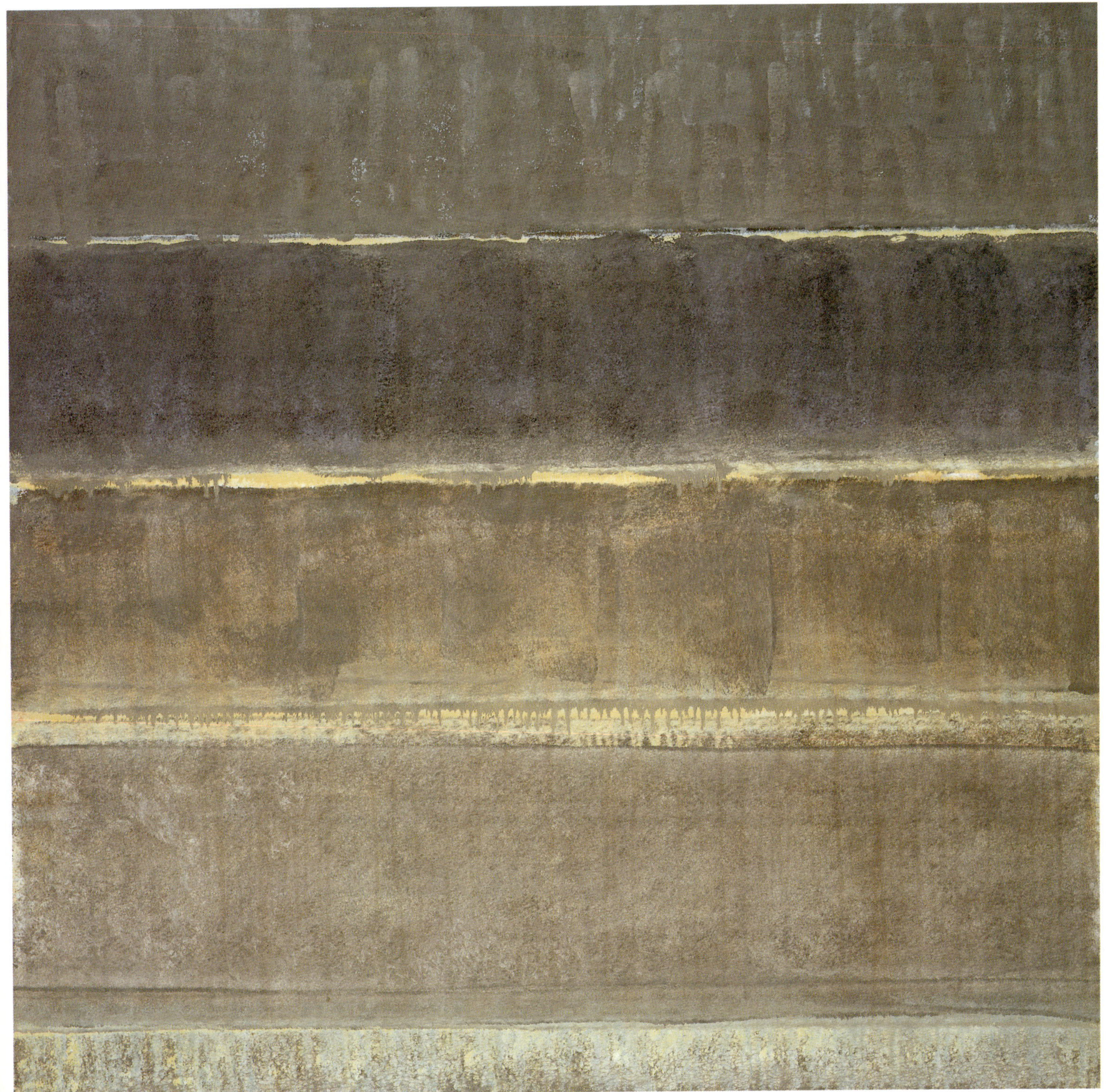

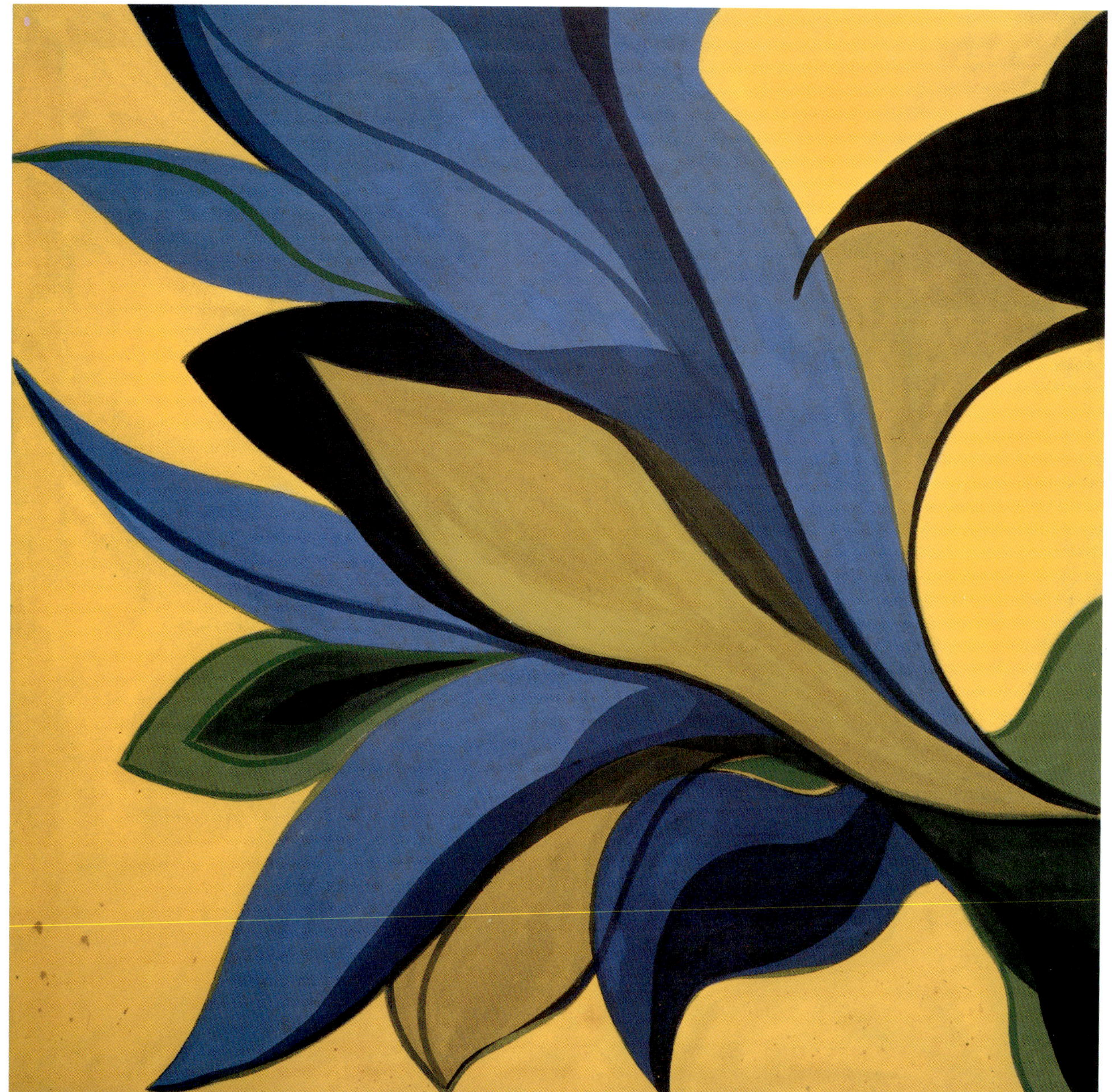

Chromatic Abstractions: Willem de Looper and the Art of Color

Blodyn, 1966
32" x 31"
acrylic on canvas
Courtesy of
The Watkins Collection
at the American University
Figure 2

Willem de Looper had his first solo exhibition in 1966 at the Jefferson Place Gallery on P Street in Washington, D.C.[1] Although he has had more than thirty solo exhibitions in the ensuing three decades in galleries from Germany to New York to St. Louis to Los Angeles, certain features of de Looper's work have remained constant, particularly his interest in abstraction and his insistence on color as his primary expressive vehicle. In this sense he is a Washington-based artist not only because he lives in D.C., but because he shares with other area artists an overriding interest in the use of color freed of any representational or pictorial responsibilities.

While such an interest in what could be termed "abstract color" is not unique to Washington, its use was prominent enough among artists in the city that in 1965 the Washington Gallery of Modern Art chose the title *Washington Color Painters* for an exhibition of the work of Morris Louis, Kenneth Noland, Gene Davis, Thomas Downing, Howard Mehring, and Paul Reed. In a sense, this was the first official recognition of the importance of color in the work of these area painters who, along with Leon Berkowitz and sculptor Anne Truitt, came to be known as the Washington Color School.

This appellation was important for the Color School artists because by the sixties, when American art occupied center stage in the international art world, "Washington Color School" (as a label) gave the work of area artists a critical identity and critical mass. In a way, the label forced Washington art to be taken seriously at a time when avant-garde art tended to be identified almost exclusively with New York. The fact that Clement Greenberg, perhaps the most influential modernist critic of the time, had, in effect, introduced Louis and Noland to the work of New York painters Jackson Pollock and Helen Frankenthaler in 1953, also helped establish the identity of Washington art.

Something that has been a point of discussion in recent years, however, is that the label "Washington Color School" problematically grouped artists with differing intentions and sensibilities together into a monolithic whole. In the work of Color School artists, sufficient distinctions were not always made between color as space, color as form, or color as geometry. Also, non-objective process-oriented color and mystically-oriented transcendental color were not always distinguished, with the result that differences in individual artists' meanings were generally overshadowed by what was seen as a shared concentration on non-objective color.

Because Willem de Looper too, had an overriding interest in color, he immediately became identified as a "second generation" Color School painter. Consequently, his work was framed in terms of the critical discourse about non-objective color of the Washington Color School. However, in de Looper's case abstract, non-objective color was indeed his central concern. In spite of the landscape associations in his work, he has always considered himself an abstract painter.

1966: STAINED FIELDS

Though de Looper has his own personal interests and sensibilities, his association with the Color School was immediately apparent from the time of his first solo exhibition. The works he exhibited were stained fields of color influenced by *Veils* and *Florals*, two series of paintings created by Morris Louis in the later fifties. Before this time, de Looper had produced a great many drawings and watercolors, filling a notebook with studies of works by Paul Klee and John Marin that he saw at The Phillips Collection (called The Phillips Gallery until 1960) where he had been working as a guard since 1959.[2] And while de Looper also became interested in the work of Arshile Gorky, which he saw in an exhibition at the Washington Gallery of Modern Art in 1963, most decisive for him was his encounter with the work of Louis that occurred soon afterward; especially important were Louis' *Florals*.[3]

The emotional intensity of Gorky's brushwork, like that of the Abstract Expressionist Gesture painters (Jackson Pollock, Willem de Kooning, Franz Kline) which initially impressed him at the Brussels World's Fair in 1958 during his military duty in the U.S. Army, ultimately proved unsuitable to his artistic temperament.[4] While he liked the Abstract Expressionists' use of bold color and their commitment to abstraction, he responded more to the cool, process-oriented works that Louis made by pouring thinned acrylic paint on unsized and unprimed canvas. Louis' new color-space, which tended to eliminate any sense of foreground/background, quickly became the inspiration for de Looper's own experiments with color and paint. He began orienting his working methods towards process—pouring, rolling, sponging and, at one point, spraying paint.

In the mid-sixties, working with acrylic paint on unsized and unprimed canvas, de Looper created his first major body of work. Drawing, which had been so prominent in his earlier landscape and figural studies, was eliminated in favor of fields of flowing color that covered the entire canvas.[5] The result, in its softly-focused quality, could be likened to the atmospheric effects of nineteenth century artists John Constable and John Turner, two artists whom de Looper much admired for their use of color. However, the color of de Looper's combinations of transparent washes are intense and bright, and have little to do with representational illusions of nature. If there is a visual connection, it results rather from the way de Looper's process orientation to materials (i.e., flowing transparent paint) parallels the luminosity Constable and Turner created by depicting light streaming through billowing clouds. Thus, while de Looper does respond to landscape (perhaps even subconsciously to that of his native Holland with its vast skies and prominent horizons), as becomes apparent in his paintings of the seventies, he is not a landscape painter in any traditional sense. Rather, he is a non-objective, avant-garde artist who, as critic Greenberg argued as early as 1939, *tries in effect to imitate God by creating something valid solely on its own terms, in the way nature itself is valid, in the way a landscape not its picture is aesthetically valid.*[6]

For de Looper, painting is connected to nature via the artist's exploitation of the natural properties of materials. Because such materials, like nature itself, are constrained by physical laws, a parallel exists between nature and painting. Nonetheless, for de Looper, painting begins with *materials*, not with representational preconceptions.

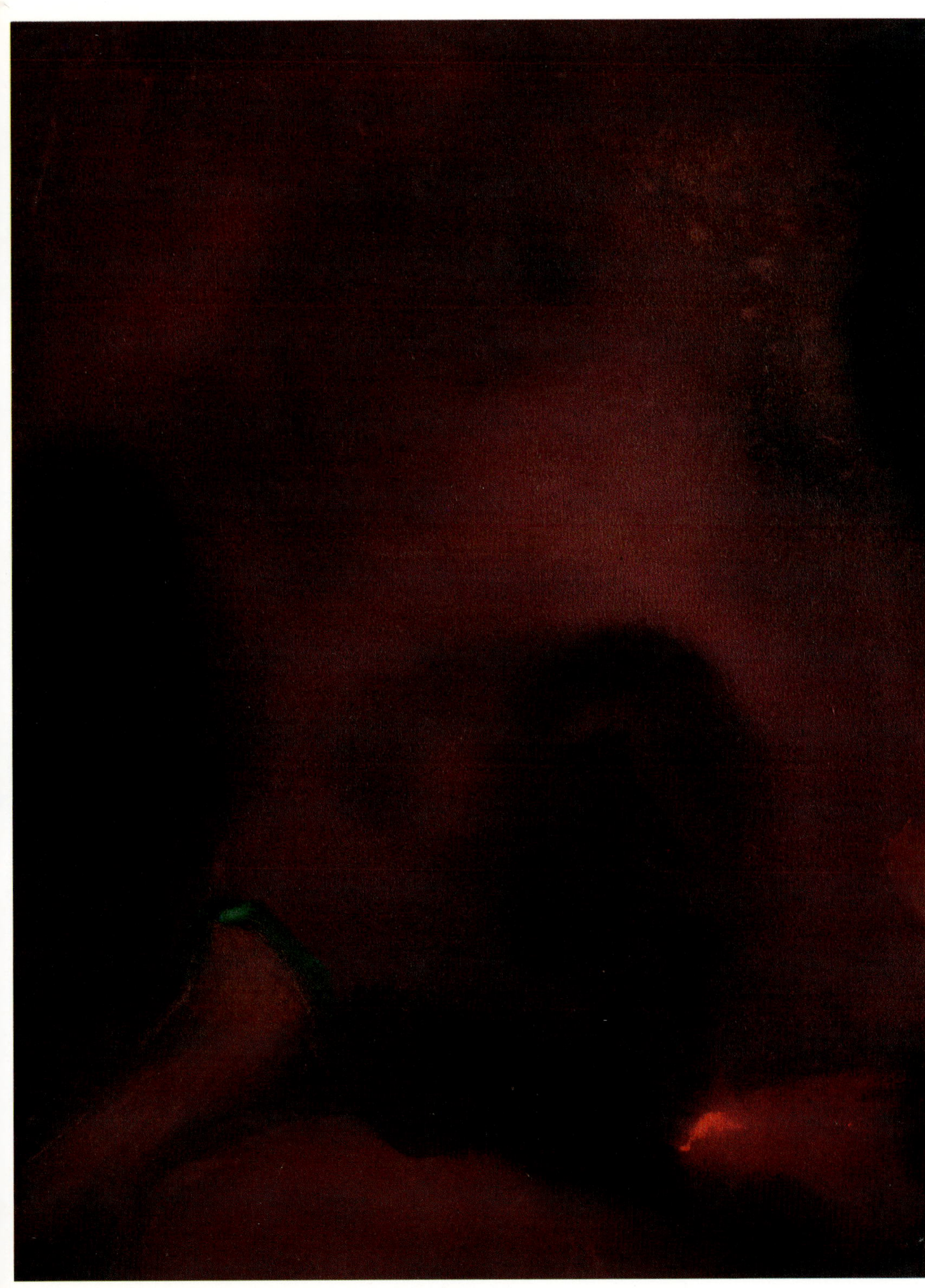

Red, 1968
24.875" x 18"
acrylic on canvas
Collection of the artist
Figure 3

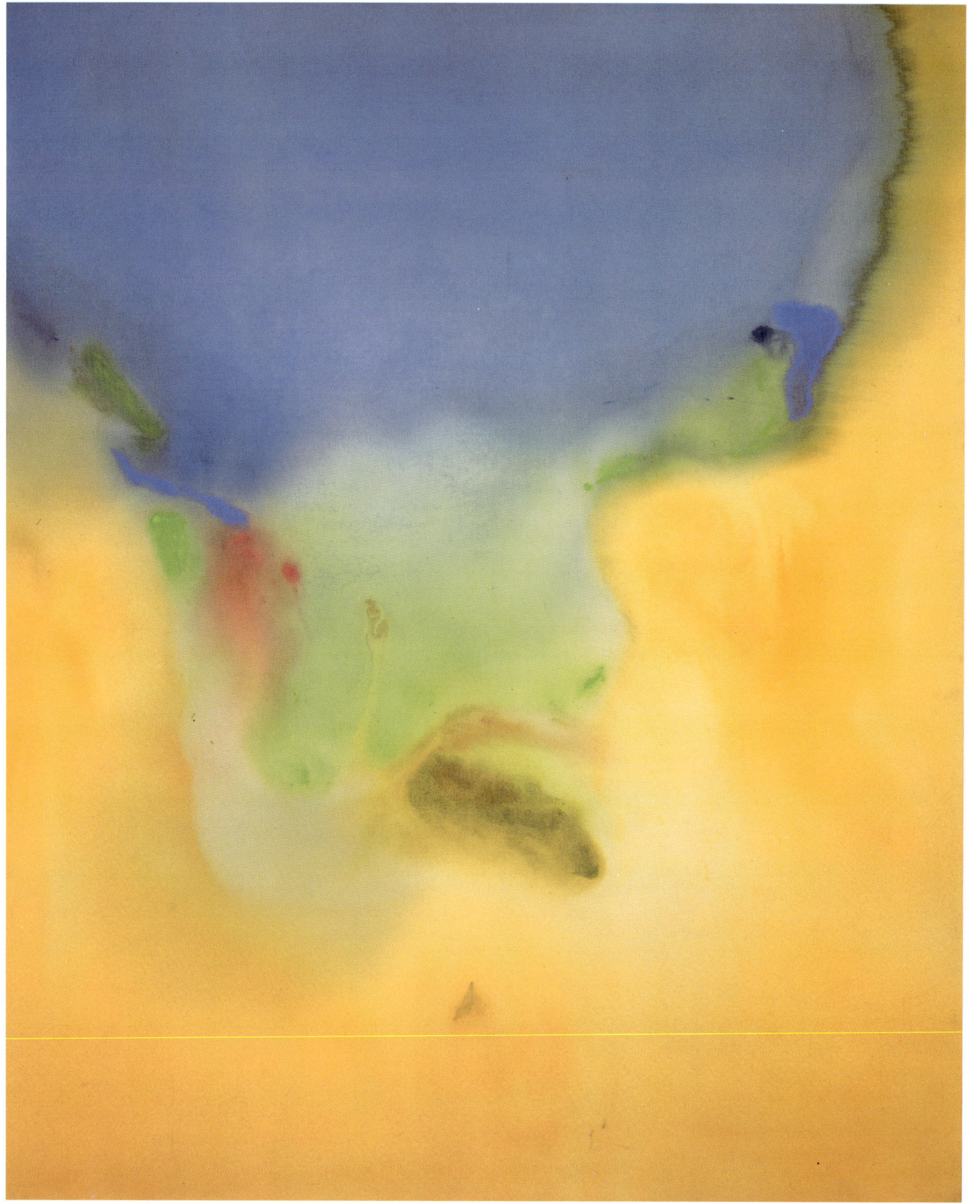

Summer, 1975
61.5" x 49"
acrylic on canvas
Collection of the artist
Figure 4

While it is obvious that the work of Louis influenced de Looper's first major body of paintings, it is important to note that by the time of his first solo exhibition in 1966, de Looper had already established his own identity. Specifically, Louis' working process and compositional structures had become more "mechanistically" pre-determined in a way that foreshadowed the Process Art of the later sixties and early seventies.[7] This is apparent in the *Unfurled* series in which Louis "discovered" drawing, so to speak, in the edges of rivulets of paint carefully poured across the corners of vast, empty canvases. In contrast, de Looper was always more intuitive, working and reworking washes of paint that covered broad areas of the canvas in a manner more akin to that of Helen Frankenthaler. However, unlike Frankenthaler, who worked on unstretched canvas, only cropping afterwards to frame certain effects or highlight certain accidental details, de Looper usually worked with stretched canvas, using the precise edges both as a structural support and as an element of resistance, something to "push" against. In fact, the reason he quickly abandoned spray painting as a process was because it offered too little resistance, allowing him to paint and repaint a large canvas in minutes.

De Looper's characteristic working methods in this period can be seen in *Summer,* a painting from 1968 (Fig. 4). An area of blue drifts downward from the top edge of the canvas, flowing into a yellow area that seems to creep upwards along the sides of the canvas. The color areas, created by manipulating wet paint into wet paint, are carefully balanced within the pre-established rectangular format, a format that imposes structure on the whole. Accents and stress marks were made with the brush while the painting was soaking wet.

This approach to structure was typical of his work, something pointed out by Washington critic Benjamin Forgey in a 1968 review that characterized de Looper's art as...*almost complete disintegration of form so that the principle formal confinement available is the rectangular edge of the painting.*[8] Two years later in another review, Forgey noted that de Looper's work...*will be consistently misunderstood and undervalued if it is interpreted solely in terms of the late Morris Louis and that of Sam Gilliam...* because for de Looper, the stretcher boundary is very important. According to Forgey,...*de Looper's is in fact an art of high risk-taking within the physical and intellectual limitations set by the rectangular canvas.*[9]

This importance of the boundary is apparent in *Syrinx* (Checklist (Cl.) 7), a 1971 painting in which deep blue seems to collect around the edges of the canvas, again emphasizing the stretcher as support and constraint. *Syrinx,* however, also signals a major shift in the direction that the artist's work would take in the seventies as internal structural elements start to develop out of the painting process.

1972: THE HORIZONTAL FORMAT

By the early seventies, de Looper had begun to move away from what he saw as the...*excessively glamorous color, smoothness of texture and restricted size of his sixties work.* Rejecting what he called his earlier...*surfaces without incident within large areas of color,* he began to create a more active and internally structured field in which drawing reappeared as an intentional element and the material texture of paint once again articulated surface.[10] The soft-focus effect of his previous staining method disappeared and his colors started to get darker as washes began to coalesce into horizontal bands.

Acquiring a larger studio in 1969 also enabled de Looper to increase the size of his works allowing him to exploit the effect of larger masses of color, something Matisse had used early in the century. All of these features are already evident in *Untitled*, a painting from August 1972 (Cl. 8). By the beginning of 1973, the horizontal bands had become zones of close-valued hues and their edges had become the junctures of complex and varied color interactions. It is as if these junctures are created by color squeezed into the crevices between bands. The thickness of the bands counterbalances the brighter or more active color where the bands join, imparting a subtle tension to the entire field.

Another telling feature of the work of the early to mid seventies is that color and color harmonies become much more complex. Even when a single color such as blue dominates a painting, creating an essentially monochromatic field as in *Untitled* from 1973 (Fig. 5), the effect is achieved by the layering of translucent paint of different hues, rather than the sole use of blue. In this, one can see the influence of Mark Rothko, a color-field artist whose works are prominent in The Phillips Collection where de Looper had been an Assistant Curator since 1972. However, again there are telling differences. Unlike Rothko, de Looper uses translucent paint that seems built up through layers of staining; he doesn't feather the edges of his colors; nor are his forms bound within the canvas. Instead he creates surface incident by various techniques including encouraging what seems to be the puddling of paint so that the edges of his bands, and color areas within bands, are ragged and have an uneven translucency. This re-introduces an aspect of drawing and gesture as a way of reasserting surface. Though dry and matte, the actual tangible quality of paint visible on the canvas has a translucency that at once creates and dispels the illusions of depth, which makes these paintings shimmer and tremble before the eye of the viewer.

There is something very American about de Looper's works of this period, which is ironic since the artist was born in Holland. However, on numerous occasions, including in a 1975 interview with Cynthia J. McCabe, de Looper has noted his longtime fascination with America that began when he was a child: *I was always interested in the U.S. Holland, in general, is a country that is culturally more attuned to the U.S. than to England, and they are very interested in English [i.e. American] books and periodicals, movies and plays. It is one of the few countries where movies are shown in English. Little things like that have a lot to do with how you grow up. Also, I love jazz, and that was one of the reasons I came here, practically. The first night I came to the U.S. I went to a club in New York.*[11]

What is particularly American about these paintings is a dualism that exists between the effects of light—its luminosity, clarity, and translucency—and the unceasing tangible presence of paint (as a material substance) on the canvas. In a gallery essay for a retrospective of de Looper's work from this period, the artist and critic Ray Kass, after commenting on the luminosity

Untitled, 1973
87.5" x 96"
acrylic on canvas
Collection of the artist
Figure 5

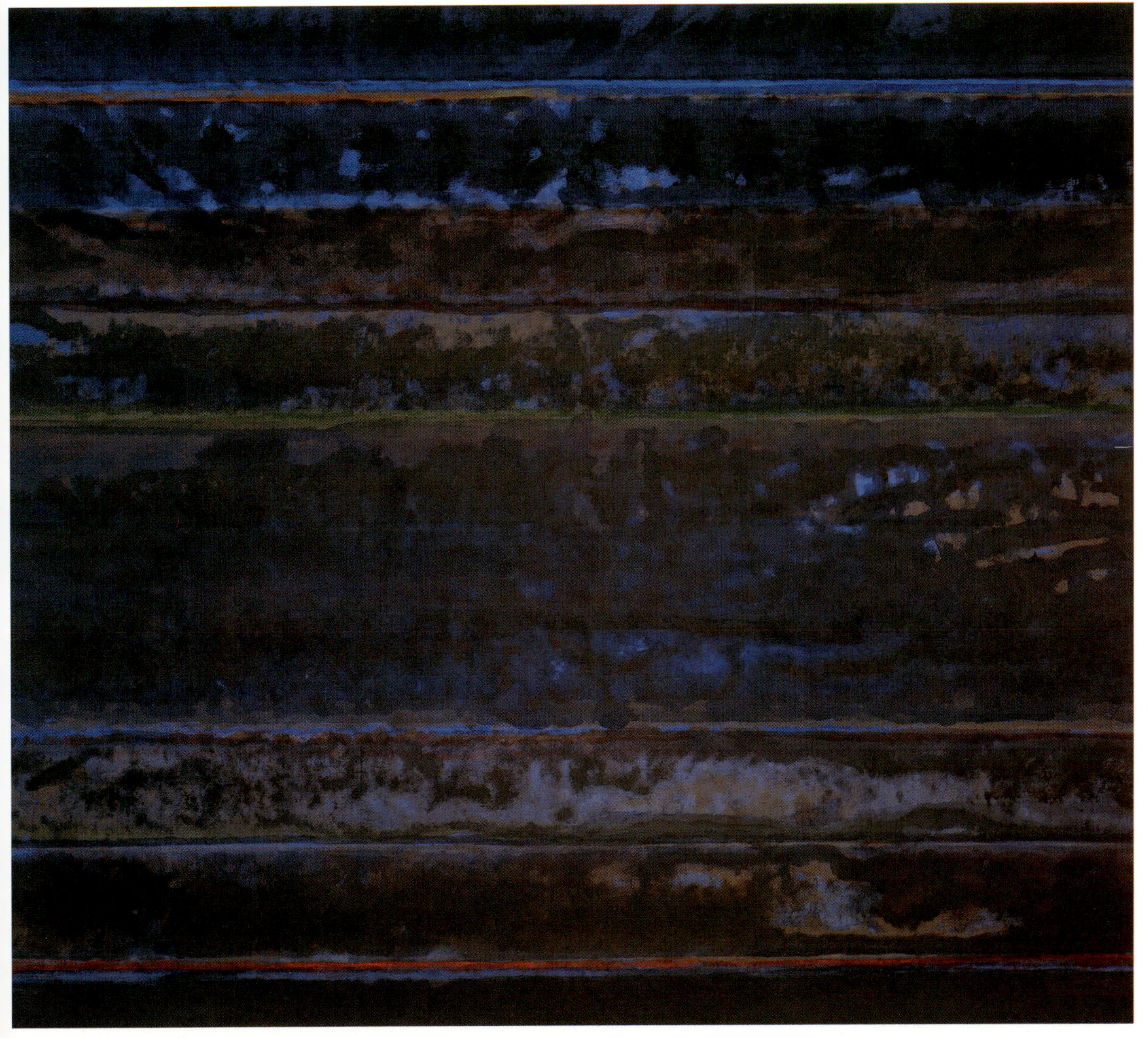

Sur, 1975
74" x 95"
acrylic on canvas
Collection of
The Phillips Collection
Figure 6

and material substance of the paintings, wrote that de Looper was committed to... *'painting' as the material means of inventing phenomenal space...his linear patterns are functionally deeper than flat grids...; they introduce a complex visual dialogue between inner and outer space which is an issue at the heart of his painting.*[12]

This dichotomy between the "inner and outer space" and the dualism in what Kass refers to as the materiality of de Looper's art, are features that American art historian Barbara Novak traced back to the colonial limner tradition of portraiture that John Singleton Copley inherited; Novak characterized this portraiture as having...*a pull toward the plane, an overall uniformity of painted surface, and an equalization of parts and linear distinctness.*[13] Novak also reads these features in the landscapes of the nineteenth century Luminist painters Fitz Hugh Lane, Martin Johnson Heade, and John F. Kensett. The parallel between luminist landscapes and this series of horizontally-formatted paintings by de Looper is the quality of light structured within...*a complex visual dialogue of inner and outer space*. According to Novak,...*luminist light largely derives its special qualities from its containment within clearly defined geometries and sometimes, too, from the opposition of its brilliance to the ultra-clarification of foreground detail.*[14]

De Looper's oeuvre from the seventies can be likened in further ways to the painting of Copley and the Luminist artists. In these paintings, de Looper creates a planar surface contained by the strict geometries of his horizontal bands while holding deep space in check, as if in opposition to the close-up texture of paint as foreground detail. In short, while painterly detail plays the dual roles of creating depth and articulating surface, it never totally succumbs to purely atmospheric or illusionistic spatial effects as often happens in the work of European Surrealists such as Matta and Tanguy.

Once de Looper established his horizontal format, he created a series of works that harmonized color into fields of steely blue, cold gray-whites, and earthy hues. The landscape and colors of the American West, an area de Looper had seen during a 1971 trip across the country to Arizona and New Mexico, were probably an influence on these works which, as critic James Mahoney wrote in *Art in America*, are a...*genuine bid to reify visual experience [of nature].*[15]

However, it would be a mistake to see his study of the colors of the landscape as the sole impetus for the new subtlety and sophistication with which de Looper handles the color harmonies in these works. They are also influenced by his longstanding interest in music, both jazz and classical. Just as the American expatriate painter Whistler explained that his "crepuscules," dreamy landscapes made by horizontal strokes, relied on color harmonies and were associated with the intrinsic abstraction of music, and employed abstraction rather than representational form to hold them together, so too has de Looper discussed the relationship between music and his own work. In a recent letter, he noted that his interest in harmony and rhythms...*likely ties in with my deep interest in music.* He went on to say that...*although my paintings are, as all painting, a distillation of nature, they are as abstract as music.*[16]

1978: GEOMETRIC PANEL PAINTINGS

The year following the closing of Jefferson Place Gallery in 1974, de Looper moved to the Max Protetch Gallery where Robert Mangold's Minimalist works were being shown. De Looper noted that their spareness began "rubbing off" on him. As a consequence of Mangold's influence, de Looper began following the work of other Minimalist artists, especially Agnes Martin and Robert Ryman, and sought out their work during his frequent trips to New York for The Phillips Collection around this time. Eventually his work evolved into the Minimalist-influenced geometric abstractions that characterize his paintings in the period beginning in the late seventies and continuing until the early eighties.

By the end of 1977, the strict horizontal format with bands bleeding off the sides of the canvas gives way as vertical bands are introduced into de Looper's compositions. What resulted are works that contained a greater degree of geometrical complexity within the compositional field as in *Untitled*, an acrylic on paper of January 1978 (Fig. 7). In general, a grid format is implied in these works as they become more formal, structure and composition become more elaborate, and the role of texture and surface incident is reduced.

However, as is typical of de Looper throughout his career, he did not totally abandon his own instincts for color and touch to substitute the then-prevalent Minimalist predilection for strict geometry and uninflected surface. As critic Cynthia Saltzman wrote in *ARTnews* about his 1979 New York show at the Sarah Y. Rentschler Gallery ...*de Looper successfully treads a stylistic border between translucent color-field painting and neater, smaller-scale geometric abstraction.*[17]

Structurally, these new works rely on the placement of one geometric form in relation to another and use a system in which the compositional weight of a form is determined by its size, value contrast, and color. This is a move away from the earlier use of complex color harmonies and texture within an almost pre-set composition of horizontal bands. Nonetheless, these new geometries, which are less busy, are never completely devoid of color harmony or touch, as Saltzman points out in her review: *Despite the sense of geometric order [in these works]..., an elusive, intangible quality emerges as their most interesting character trait. One picks up the subtle instability from the arrangement of shapes. The stained rectangles, instead of being locked into a surface pattern bound by hard edges, have tentative, wobbling borders.*[18]

These "wobbling borders" are intentional. Purposely done without using masking tape, forms are rendered "free hand" to give their edges an irregular contour that reinforces the sense of the handmade apparent in the uneven, patinated color within. Also, the rectangles are usually separated or outlined by threads of contrasting color which not only inflect upon the hue of the surrounding rectangular fields, but emphasize the human touch of the artist through drawing.

The idea of a pure, absolute geometry is simply foreign to these works. In their muted, often close-value color combinations, they continue the "quietist" mood of the earlier works, but with a new sense of

Untitled, 1978
21.75" x 21.75"
acrylic on canvas
Collection of the artist
Figure 7

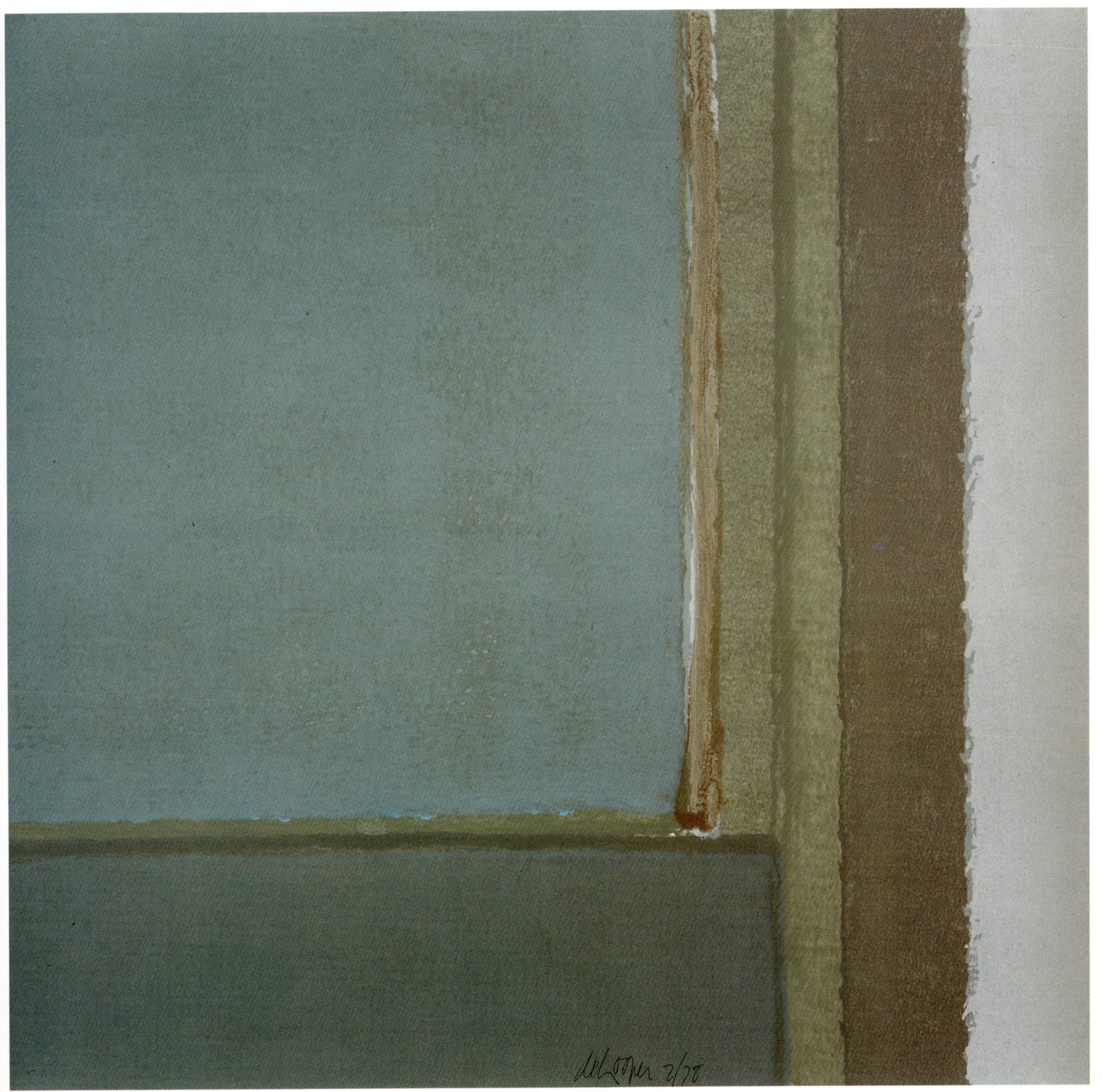

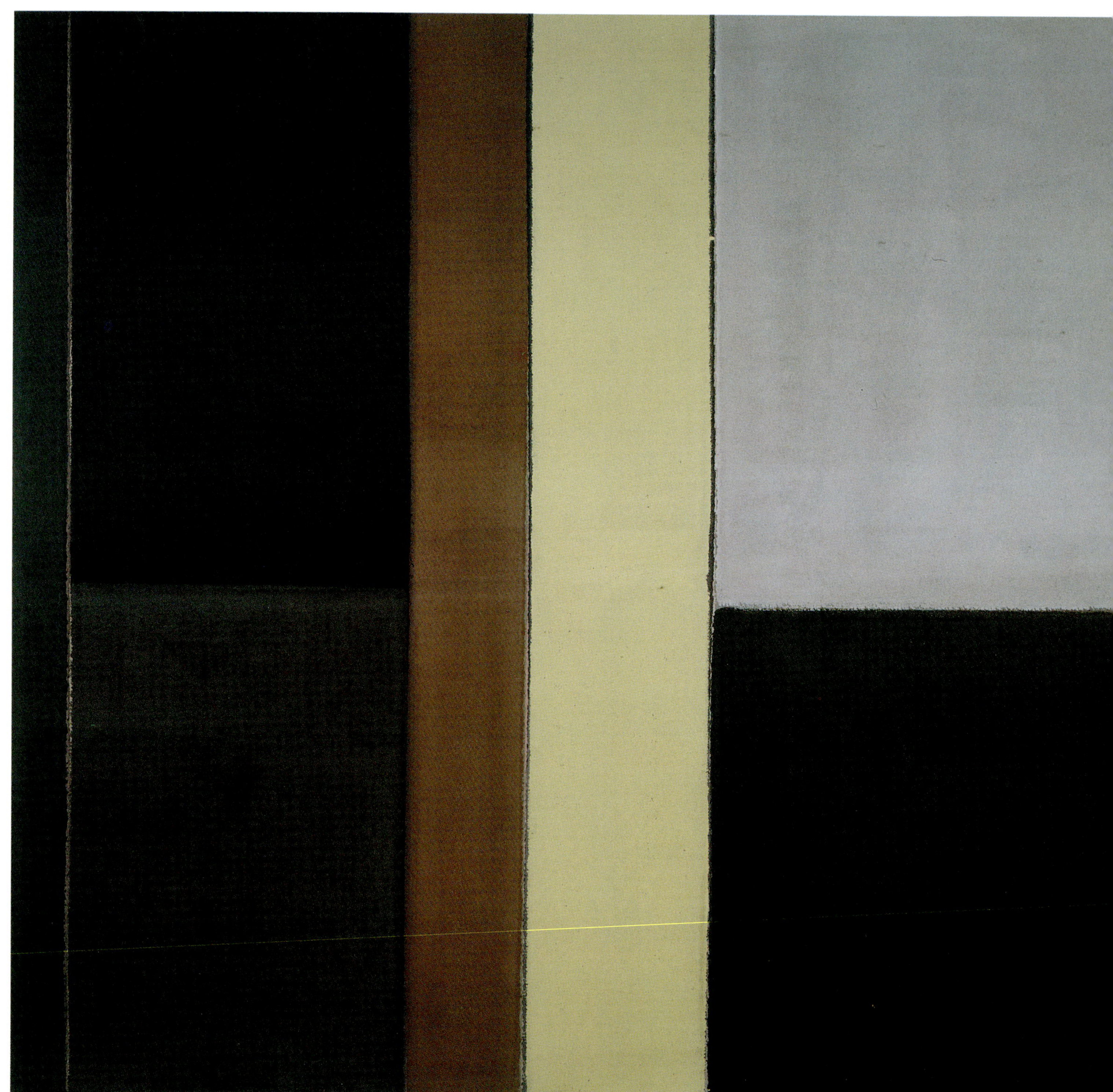

II, 1980
72" x 96"
acrylic on canvas
Collection of the artist
Figure 8

constructed, man-made space. Unlike the earlier images in which space evokes associations with landscape through texture and color harmonies, de Looper's new space seems more related to architecture. The interiors of Edouard Vuillard, the French painter whose small, intimate domestic scenes are some of the jewels of The Phillips Collection, come to mind. Many of de Looper's small abstractions of 1979, in their palette of brown, beige, and cream, suggest a Vuillard influence. Even in the larger works, many of which are polyptychs, the spatial construction evokes something of Vuillard's cropping of corners, walls, doors, and windows, all of which have been arranged parallel to the picture plane. The traces of such a sensibility are evident in works like the one from 1979 in the Corcoran collection (Cl. 23) and *II* of June 21, 1980 (Fig. 8). In these works, as in so many from this period, there is a feeling of soft light filtering into a quiet interior place where the edges of forms seem tempered by familiarity and use, a place where even the slightest change would not go unnoticed.

This sensibility continues even into the early eighties when de Looper organizes his architectonic elements around what critic Jane Addams Allen described as a... *window-like structure with a large roughly rectangular central area surrounded by angular lines.*[19] De Looper adds variety to this new format by increasingly introducing curved lines.[20] At times, his lines tend to curve downward dividing a section of a central rectangle into two parts as in *Untitled,* 1980 (Fig. 9). More often, the curved lines become upward arcs that counter the more staid rectangles as in the enormous painting of 1981 (Cl. 25), a diptych organized around a centralized window-like rectangle in each panel.

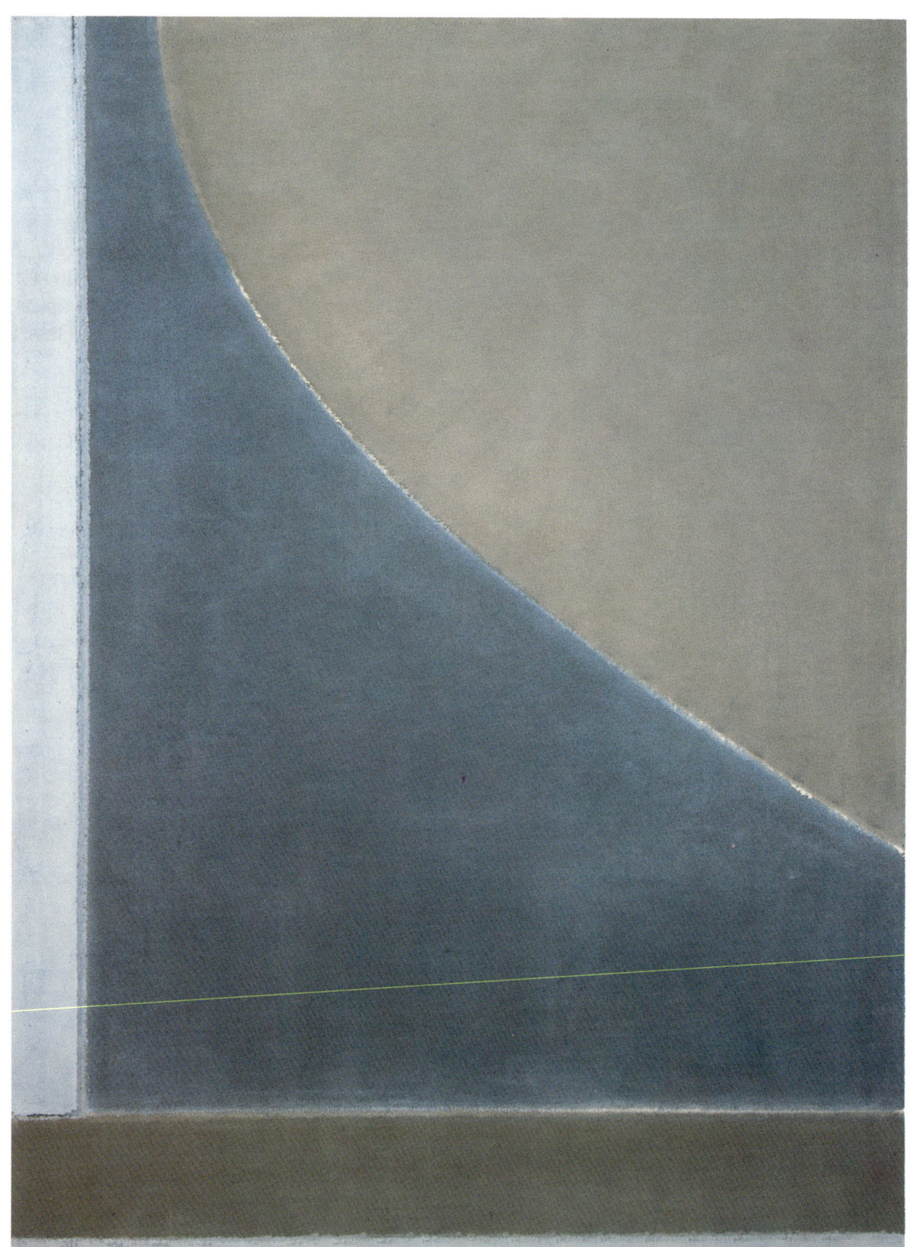

Untitled, 1980
72" x 50"
acrylic on canvas
Collection of the artist
Figure 9

In this diptych, the arced forms provide a rhythmic counterpoint to the more measured vertical rectangles they slice through. The dominant blue field of the painting resonates with verticals of various shades of blue and gray which are highlighted by lines of yellow, pink, and red that in turn echo the arcs. Other works use the window-like format but tend to rely on more muted colors—beige, cream, and a dusty desert blue—as in *Tunis*, a large work of 1983 (Cl. 20). De Looper painted this work while his wife was on a trip to North Africa to visit family friends, and thus registered his indirect experience of Tunisia; the painting also relates to Dizzy Gillespie's famous jazz composition *Night in Tunisia*, a piece de Looper knew well.[21] In 1988 this painting became the basis for a print commissioned by the Smithsonian Institution to be sold in conjunction with a fundraising effort.

The intimacy that de Looper achieves in these works has little to do with the art world's fashionable trends and novelties of the time which were often lumped together under the rubric of Neo-Expressionism. Celebrated as the "return of painting from the land of the dead," Neo-Expressionism, was loosely characterized by the use of painterly gesture, strong color, and representational subject matter. As the aesthetic quality of de Looper's paintings attest, however, Neo-Expressionism was less the return of painting to significance, than to renewed mainstream attention. In Germany it was seen as a continuation of the Expressionist painting that the Nazis condemned in the Entartete Kunst (Degenerate Art) exhibition of 1937. Because the abrupt halt in the development of Modern German Expressionist painting occurred for political reasons, the work of a host of German Neo-Expressionist artists, including Anselm Kiefer, Jorg Immendorf, Rainer Fetting, and Helmut Middendorf, is infused with genuine political meaning derived from subject matter as well as style. In Italy, Neo-Expressionism and the "revival of painting" was associated with what critic Achille Bonito Oliva termed the "Transavanguardia" and is represented by the work of artists such as Enzo Cucchi, Francesco Clemente, and Sandro Chia. In America, Neo-Expressionism was associated with Julian Schnabel and David Salle, among others.

At their best, those works labeled Neo-Expressionist were a serious engagement with the political culture surrounding art of the Modernist period. At their worst, they were an appropriation of images from what has been called the "dustbin of history"—the term "dustbin" referring to images and styles that were no longer seen as part of a truly living tradition, a life-world filled with meaning. Rather, the appropriated images were used as so many props with which to adorn one's art.

In contrast to this Neo-Expressionist attitude which became so pervasive in the decade of the eighties, de Looper maintained a deeply felt belief in art; this belief is grounded in his enduring interest in art history and reflects de Looper's confidence in art's ability to enrich, in a profound way, the life of the viewer. Because of this, the works he painted in these years were never tempted by the noise around him. Instead they seem to fuse earlier Color School ideas with the "intimate" aesthetic seen in a Vuillard interior and, perhaps, even the serenity felt in a Giorgio Morandi still life.

1983: THE NEW DECORATION

In August of 1982, de Looper's status at The Phillips Collection changed from that of Acting Curator, a position he had held since the death of Curator James McLaughlin in January, to Curator. (He had been named Associate Curator in 1974.) Now, as Curator of The Phillips Collection came the added responsibility of the museum's exhibition programs. During the next two years de Looper was involved in curating numerous small and large exhibitions including a major retrospective of the work of Morris Graves. This exhibition, with a catalogue by Ray Kass, opened at The Phillips in 1983 and then traveled to five other cities.[22] De Looper also helped organize the *Masterpieces of The Phillips Collection,* an exhibition of Impressionist and Post-Impressionist works chosen from the collection to be exhibited in Japan.

All this occupied much of his time, including much of his studio time. Furthermore, in 1979 the Max Protetch Gallery became the Protetch-McIntosh Gallery and, when Protetch moved to New York in the fall of 1981, de Looper found himself without gallery representation in Washington for the first time since 1966. These disruptions in his normal working situation resulted in the production of fewer paintings than was usual for him.

However, in November of 1983 when de Looper began to exhibit with the BR Kornblatt Gallery, it became apparent that a new direction was developing in his work. Color moved away from its associations with the natural world, not only due to the introduction of metallic paint, but also because the color he used was brighter and exhibited a greater range of contrasting hues and decorative combinations of patterning. The new color scheme and decorative patterning reflects the influence of Matisse, especially of works like *Egyptian Curtain*, (1948), and *Studio, Quai-St. Michel,* (1916-17). Both paintings have been in The Phillips Collection for many years. Typical of Matisse and important for de Looper at this time are the use of large areas of color, strong and unusual color combinations, and decorative patterns as in the red bedspread with a silver-gray flower pattern in *Studio*; also important are the black and red color scheme and blue, yellow, and green linear foliage design of *Egyptian Curtain*.

Compositionally, the architectonic structure of verticals and horizontals punctuated with curves that formed the basis of de Looper's earlier work begins to give way to rectangles placed at angles to the frame. Fields of decorative texture made by repeated patterns of line drawing also appear. According to Benjamin Forgey who reviewed the exhibition in *The Washington Post*: *Freely painted lines, often of the most brilliant hues, play tellingly across the surface, sometimes to reinforce basic forms or planes, sometimes in counterpoint to them, and sometimes to make totally independent patterns*.[23]

The new freedom seen in these works is evident in both their rendering and composition. Instead of squares and rectangles, triangular forms jut into the canvas, forming wedges of intense, bright color—greens, blues, and reds highlighted by black—that are then outlined with equally intense contrasting colors. Typical of this period are works such as the one illustrated in Figure 17 from 1985 (not in exhibition-NIE), in which a large blue triangle set askew to the bottom of the picture pushes upwards against a tripartite field of gray, green, and copper; loosely painted "parallel" lines enhance the colors of the field while animating the picture's formal elements.

The new compositional format eschews the stable, anchored forms of the earlier architectonic works. Vertical and horizontal elements disappear as de Looper now activates his compositions by using irregular shapes as dominant forms. Often set askew against the center of the picture, these shapes are "anchored" against a field built up of decorative patterns of impasto lines as in *Untitled* (Fig. 10) 1985.

As loose as the works of this period are in their details, there is still an overall tautness in their compositions—nothing is arbitrary, nothing is out of place. The assuredness of de Looper's sense of placement, color, and form remains. What has been added is a greater interest in decorative counterpoint.

The origins of this new work, with its intuitive feel, greater energy, and decorative patterns in bright color, are rather complex. They certainly relate somewhat to the drawings in watercolor and gouache that de Looper had been doing since his student days. These works were always more in the nature of quick sketches, which explains their looser, more spontaneous quality. However, these drawings were never meant as preparatory sketches for "finished" paintings. It is curious then, that their qualities should be suddenly reflected at this particular moment in his larger, more "serious" paintings.

Untitled, 1985
78" x 100"
acrylic on canvas
Collection of the artist
Figure 10

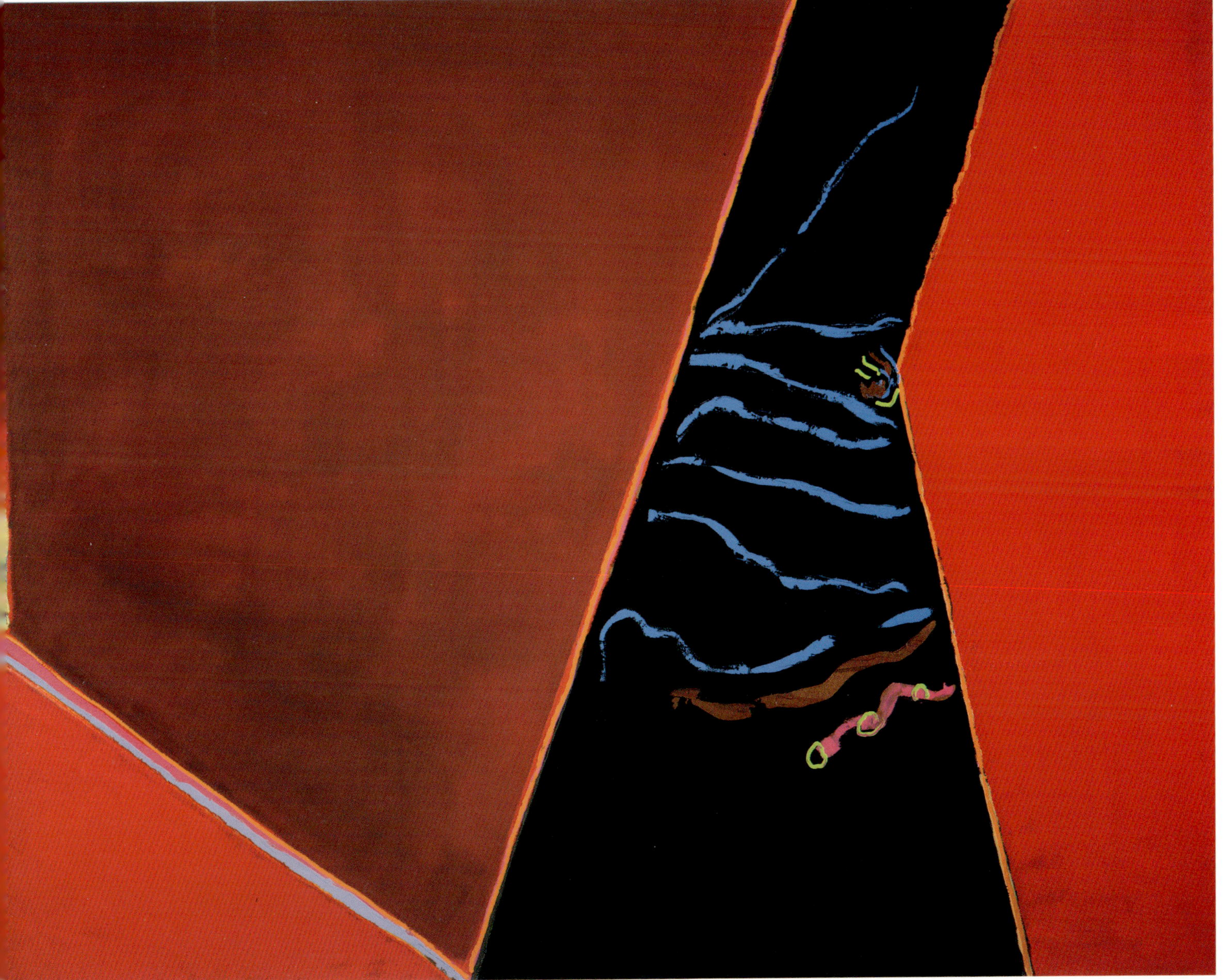

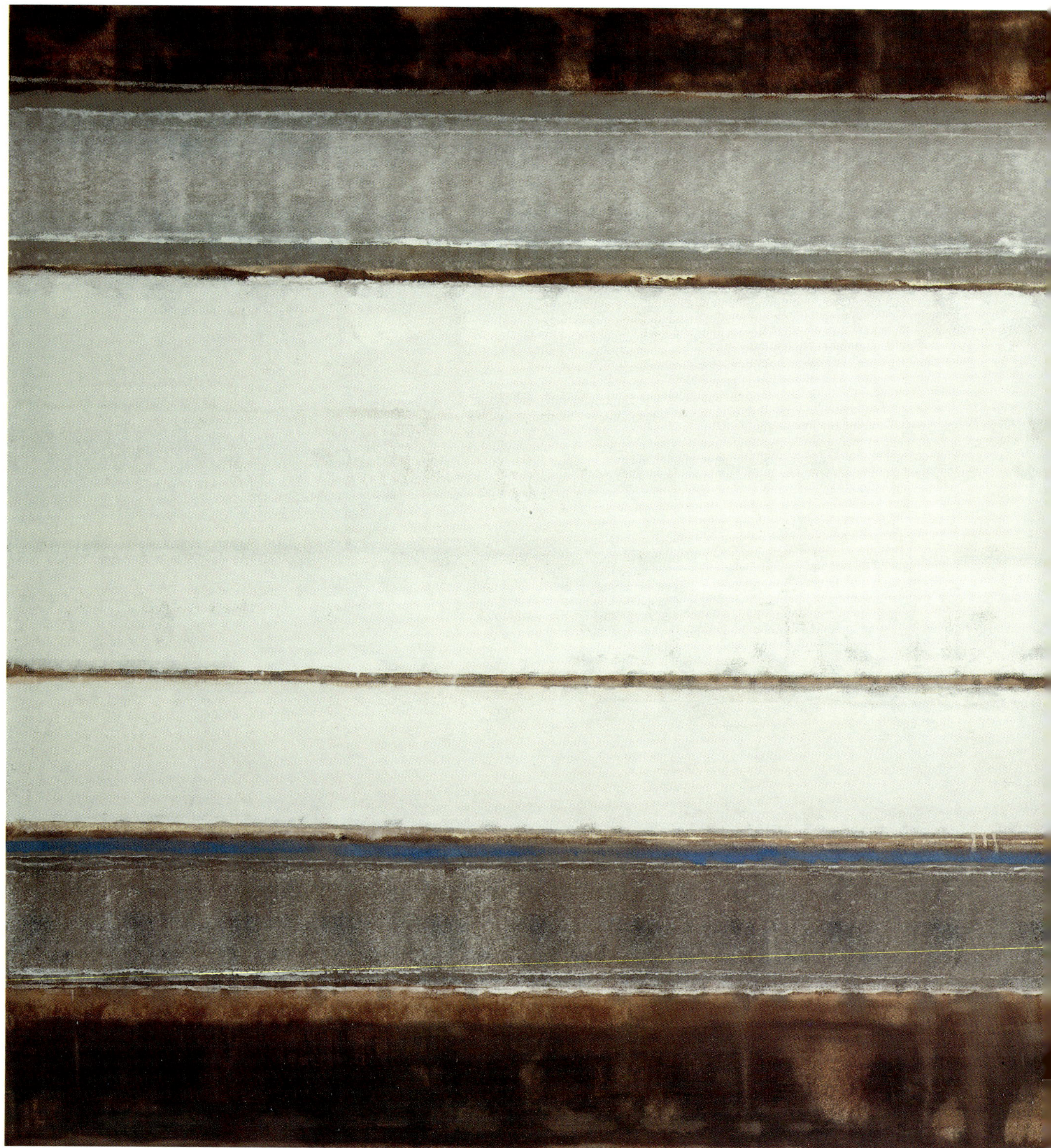

Untitled, 1975
77" x 101"
acrylic on canvas
Courtesy of
The Hirshhorn
Museum and
Sculpture Garden
Figure 11

As exhibition curator, de Looper accompanied the *Masterpieces of The Phillips Collection* to Japan in 1983 and remained there for a three-week stay. This trip was of major importance in shaping the new work of the early eighties. However, when piecing together de Looper's comments and what appears in specific paintings made at various times, it seems clear that the trip affected de Looper in at least two phases. Initially, the prospect itself of the trip seems to have triggered memories of an earlier journey de Looper and his wife Frauke made in 1977. On that occasion, they had taken a trans-Siberian railroad trip which included a stop in Japan. More important for the new work than either the stop in Japan or the crossing of the Russian expanse, however, seems to have been a side-trip to the cities of Tashkent and Samarkand in the Uzbek areas of what was then the southern reaches of the Soviet Union. As de Looper recalled in a recent conversation, the profusion of decorative designs and patterns on the Islamic architecture, as well as the bright blue turbans worn by the inhabitants of these cities, made a strong impression on him—as did the arches of the local architecture to which he attributes the curves that appeared in his paintings around 1980. Apparently, just as it took several years of exhibiting alongside the Minimalist artists at the Protetch Gallery before their influence began to reach him, so too with some of these Islamic impressions; they must have remained buried deep in his artistic memory until the prospect of the 1983 trip to Japan almost six years later began to awaken them.

While influences are never absolutely discrete in de Looper's work because of his keen interest in art from all periods and cultures, the second phase of influence from this 1983 trip appears in work produced after his return in October of that year. De Looper traces his use of metallic paints, foils, and the diptych and triptych "screen" formats to works of art he encountered on the trip.[24] However, he also mentioned in conversation that while traveling to Germany on business for The Phillips Collection in 1985, he visited Florence, where he was equally impressed by Early Italian Renaissance paintings, especially their bright colors and gilding.

1987:WINDOWS: THE "RECTANGLE WITHIN RECTANGLE" FORMAT

In 1987, de Looper resigned as Curator at The Phillips Collection. Although he worked on several more shows as Consulting Curator, a title he held until 1994, his last exhibition as Curator was *John Graham: Artist and Avatar* in 1987.[25] His retirement left him more time for studio work. In February of 1988, he had a solo exhibition at the Shippee Gallery in New York.[26] The works in this exhibition, titled *Windows*, again show a change in direction. The decorative patterns, irregular forms, and thick, opaque paint of the previous works are replaced with a renewed expansiveness. At first glance, these new paintings are reminiscent of Robert Motherwell's *Open Series* in which a small drawn or painted rectangle interrupts a large field of color so as to articulate space and inflect on the field's color. On closer inspection, however, the connection to Motherwell proves to be true only on a superficial level. In de Looper's works, the rectangle—which sometimes is centered in the middle of the field, but more often enters the field from the top edge of the canvas—is larger, creating a greater balance with the field around it. In this way, the rectangular form doesn't so much interrupt the field as appear to be inserted into the field. Also, the careful treatment of the edges between the rectangle and the surrounding field (sometimes the white of the canvas shows, other times a bright color shows) distinguishes these two areas of the painting. This approach to the edges prevents any suggestion of overlapping and forces the field into equilibrium around the rectangle, almost as a framing element.

These works from the late eighties recall the window-like format of those from the start of the decade; the later paintings also have something of the earlier one's simplicity, not only compositionally, but also in terms of their reduced surface incident or lack of painterly gesture. The surrounding fields tend to be areas of monochromatic color applied with a roller. Any texture, surface incident, or changes in tone usually result from the movement of the roller. By contrast, the centralized rectangles are often filled with overlapping veils of strong color created by pouring paint. The return to the staining technique of earlier years gives a wonderful luminosity to the central areas of these paintings, a luminosity that is accentuated by the way de Looper carefully edges the rectangle with lines of bright, intense color.

The balanced serenity seen here soon shifted and a sense of greater tension emerged. In *Untitled* dated November 10, 1988 (Cl. 34), a basically square field of black has an equally dark square, outlined in bright red, inserted into it. Within this small square is a broad, curving band of copper paint with a rippling surface resulting from the roller.[27] The gravitational pull of this "swipe" moving upwards across the interior square, fills this area with a tension that the initial works in the series do not

Untitled, 1987
78" x 100"
acrylic on canvas
Collection of the artist
Figure 12

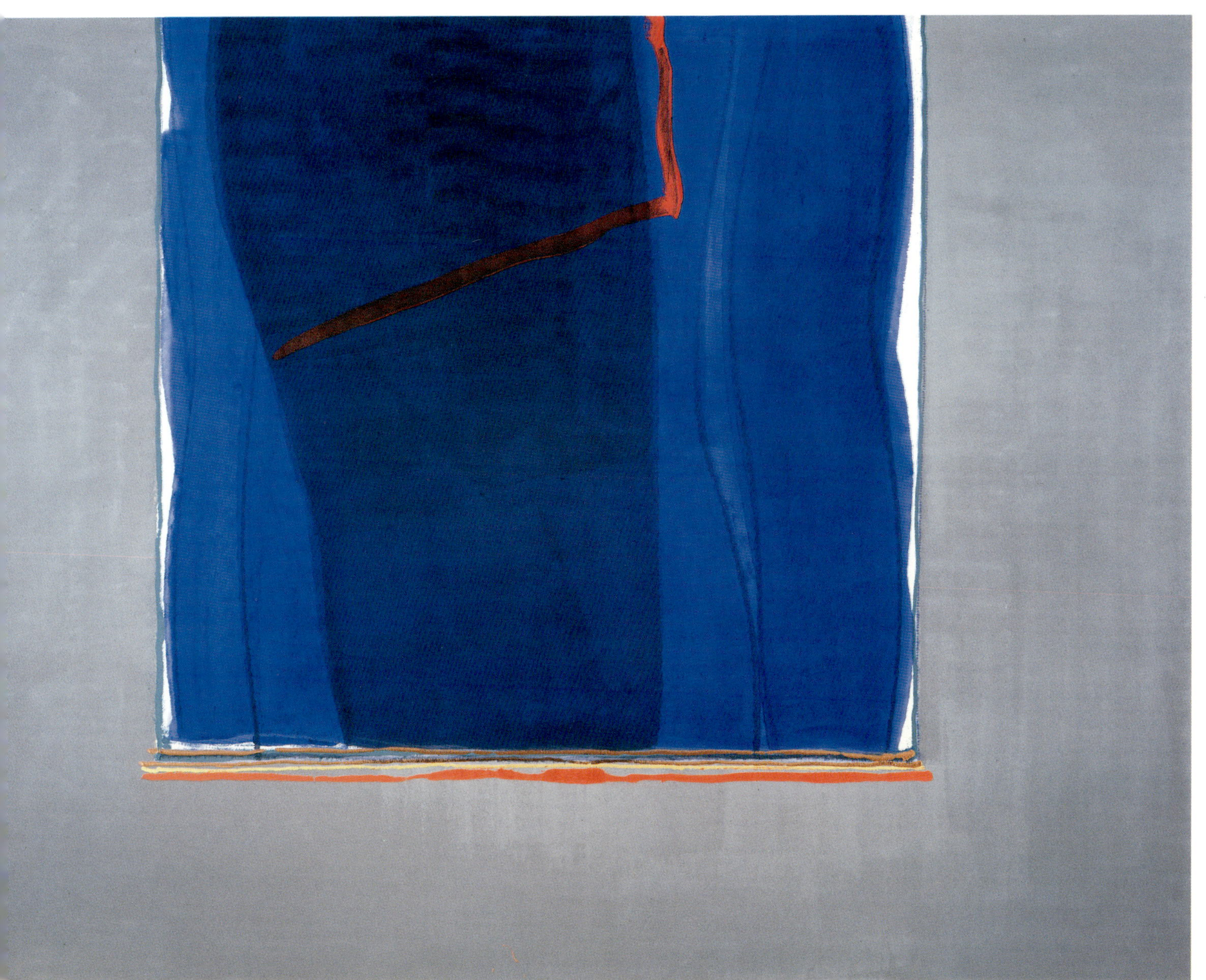

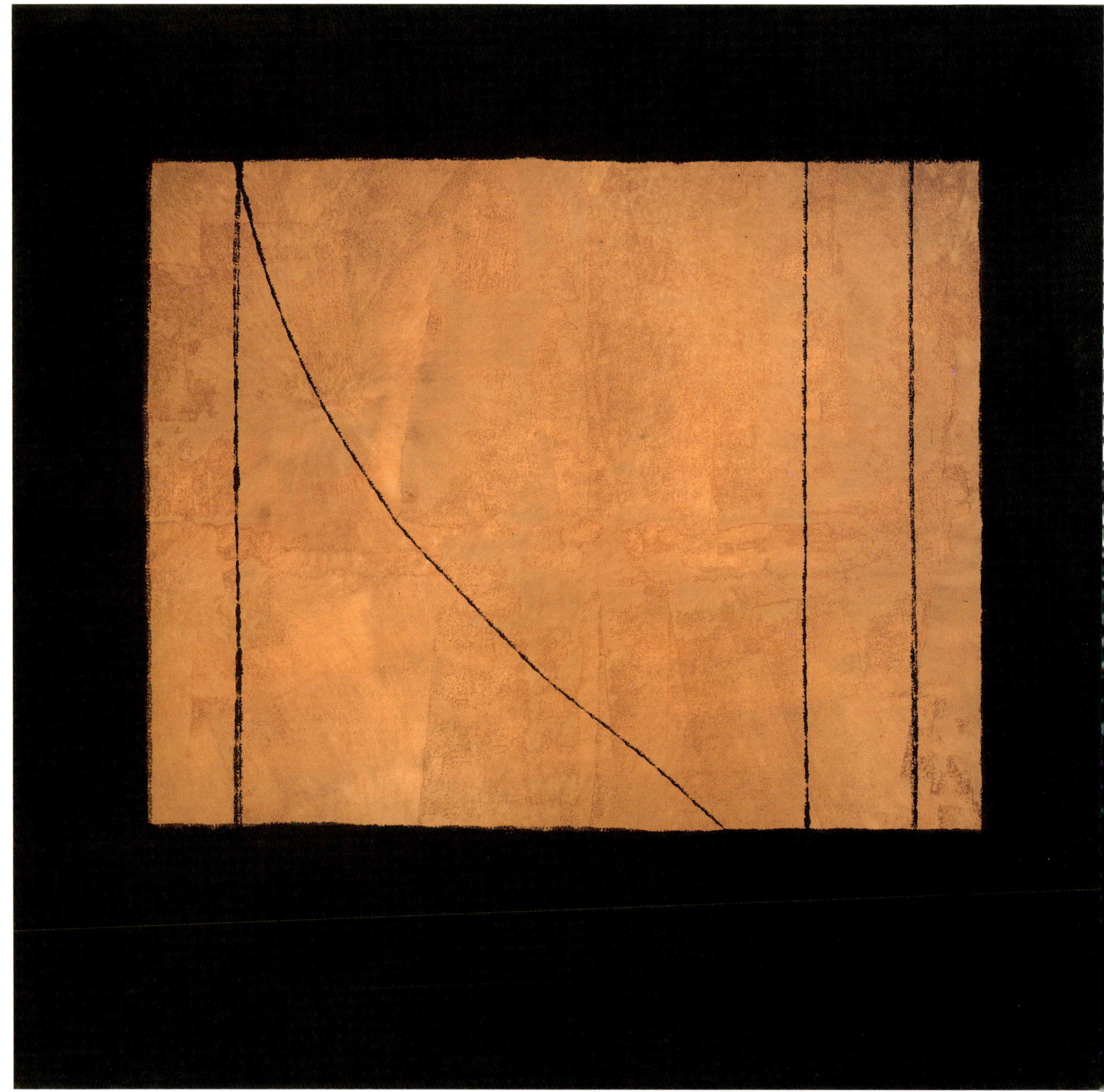

have. Equilibrium in the earlier works was achieved with an air of serenity; in this painting, equilibrium exists, but serenity gives way to balance under tension.

De Looper continued to develop the "rectangle within rectangle" format with varying degrees of complexity in 1989 and well into the nineties. A 1989 painting has an inserted form shifted to the right so that it is framed on only two sides by the field. This shifting introduces a new element as does the use of a translucent metallic paint with pearlescent toning which is rolled on so as to purposely leave bold directional marks. The result is a painting which displays tension as well as luminosity.

In a similar but compositionally less complex work, *Paso Doble*, a square painting of 1993 (Fig. 13), a copper square of denser paint is centered within a black field. Framed on all sides, almost as if it were matted, the copper square is marked with thin black lines that articulate vertical bands. These elements are tied together by a line that gently curves from upper left to bottom right. In contrast to this work is *East* of August 1988 (NIE). While the basic "rectangle within rectangle" is still visible, the overall appearance of *East* is more involved. The framing elements change colors and break into the central rectangle, more surface incident and texture are evident, and the spatial configurations are much more complex. Similar complexity characterizes *East West Encounter* of 1994 (Cl. 46). In this diptych the space becomes layered through the use of a large white field into which the rectangle is inserted. Both areas are divided into rectilinear shapes cut by curved lines. Parts of the resulting shapes are left white while others are painted red or black. The "rectangle within rectangle" format still exists, but it is more implied than visibly articulated; the overall effect is that of a ghostly image resonating within a ghostly field.

Paso Doble, 1993
72" x 72"
acrylic on canvas
Collection of the artist
Figure 13

1988: THE NEW SPATIAL COMPLEXITY

As the titles *East* and *East West Encounter* indicate, de Looper's art in the 1980s was influenced by his experiences of Asia. As just described, these works use the "rectangle within rectangle" format, but they also show something of the richness of color seen in paintings from around 1983-1985—that is, the works influenced by the visit to Tashkent and Samarkand. The new spatial complexity of *East* and *East West Encounter* however, is more directly related to a series of works that de Looper began in the late fall and the early winter of 1988. These 1988 paintings, organized around a window structure that echoes the "rectangle within rectangle" format, may be a reinterpretation of influences from his trip to Japan in 1983. Most likely, they also were influenced by the Italian Renaissance paintings seen two years later in Florence.

The color scheme of the 1988 series relies on thick paint (often applied with a palette knife), and much black, gold, and silver. They have a burnished look recalling Early Italian Renaissance gilding as well as Japanese screen paintings. A particularly good example of this influence is *Untitled* (Fig. 14, NIE) exhibited at the Kornblatt Gallery in the spring of 1989.[28] While this work still features traces of the "rectangle within rectangle" format, it also strongly suggests the Renaissance triptych and the Japanese folding screen formats because of its division into three zones of dark-valued color. The central zone is black, while the flanking zones are gold and silver placed against dark green areas which hug the perimeter of the canvas. Some of the areas are punctuated with bright red line work. The painting has a burnished, aged quality that evokes precious objects—gilded paintings, folding screens, lacquered statues, and objects of ritual use—the kinds of objects preserved in museums in Florence and temples in Nara, the eighth century capital of Japan that de Looper visited in 1983.[29]

In the later works in this series, rectangles arranged vertically and diagonally, create complex structures—formal configurations of what appear to be layered planes. Because the planes are all arranged parallel to the picture surface, they defeat any suggestion of traditional illusionism. For example, in a painting from December 1988, the seemingly layered planes are articulated and separated from each other by contrasting finishes, textures, and colors. Thus, they appear to all lay on the same surface. Because the rectangles are cropped by the picture edges, these paintings suggest large-scale Cubist-type grids that extend beyond the frame. Due to the skillful organization of the rectangles, they seem to crop each other, configuring and re-configuring in the mind's eye as attention continually shifts from one to the other in a kind of whirling, pinwheel fashion. The visual organization of these forms clearly owes something to the early Cubist works of Picasso, Braque, and Juan Gris. That de Looper should title one of his 1995 works *Homage to B* (the "B" refers to Braque) is not surprising.

Through unstable figure-ground relationships, de Looper fabricates a spatial logic in these works that seems totally at odds with the poise and serenity of the paintings of early 1987 shown at the Shippee Gallery in New York. The expansiveness and tranquility of the 1987 paintings with their ringing luminosity succumbs to an intellectually-charged space filled with visual and psychological tension. The post-1988 paintings acquire this tension because the precisely constructed forms suggest order, even an architectonic order, which is then undercut by the viewer's inability to establish perceptual stability. Because of the way the forms are constructed and arranged, the viewer is unable to prevent them from continually reconfiguring into new compositions. The result is reminiscent of Japanese paintings of architectural scenes, scenes in which glimpses into rooms are severely cropped at oblique angles by slab-like roof lines. Gone is the quiet simplicity of Vuillard, and in its place is a composition of high tension and instability, something more akin to courtly intrigue than domestic bliss.

These paintings are the most spatially complex and intellectually dense that de Looper has created and their influence is visible in much of the work that follows, most obviously in the color and complexity of paintings such as *Untitled* from 1989 (Cl. 36) with its black, brown, silver, and white color scheme and its pinwheel formal organization. Another work directly related to this series is *The Duke* (Fig. 16) from 1989.

THE RECENT WORK

Since his student days, the artist has been in the habit of filling sketchbooks with drawings and paintings. During trips for The Phillips Collection, working in such books was a way for de Looper to record impressions and places and to keep inventing while away from the studio.

Untitled, 1988
48" x 72"
acrylic on canvas
Collection of the artist
Figure 14

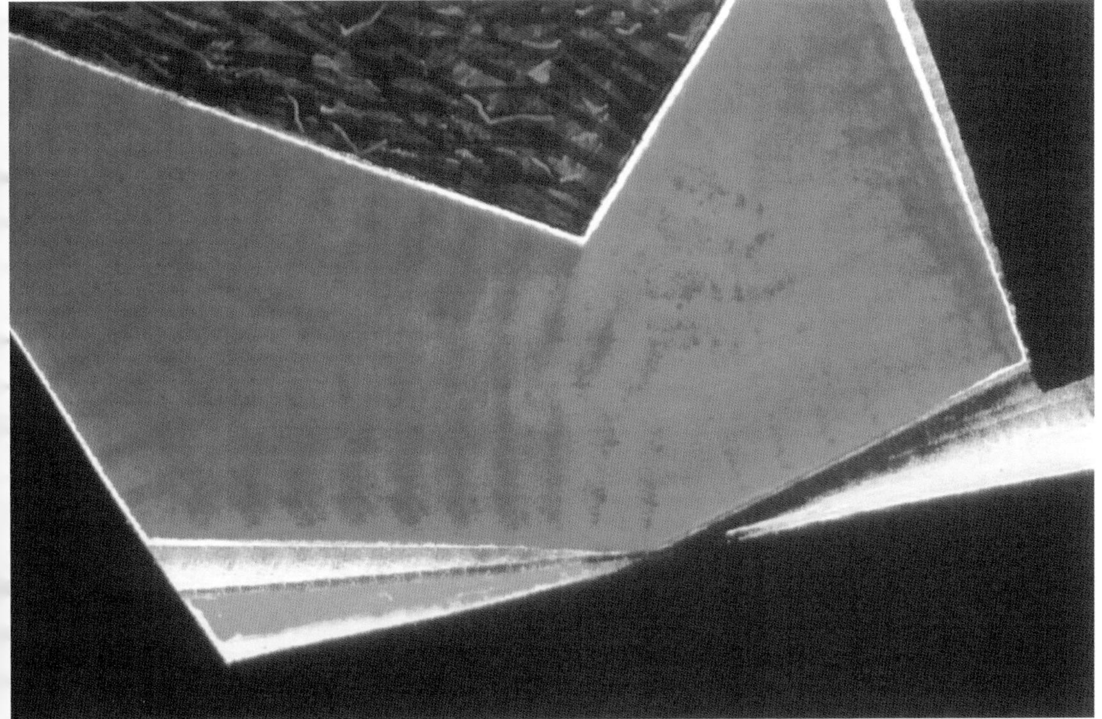

Black Mesa, 1992
48" x 72"
acrylic on canvas
Courtesy of Atrium Gallery,
St. Louis
Figure 15

The Duke, 1989
80" x 60"
acrylic on canvas
Courtesy of Atrium Gallery, St. Louis
Figure 16

Some of these small works and books were first exhibited in 1978 at the Jean Marie Antone Gallery in Baltimore. In 1989, the Jones Troyer Fitzpatrick Gallery exhibited a selection of works in watercolor, acrylic, and gouache taken from these books at the same time that the Kornblatt Gallery exhibited larger paintings on canvas and board.

These concurrent exhibitions provided an important opportunity to compare the small and large works. What became clear immediately was that the small images represented an approach that differed from that used in the large paintings. Perhaps because of their small size, the artist felt able to experiment to a greater degree. Much looser and improvisatory in nature, works from the sketchbooks display an inventiveness of form and color that seldom falters. Their intimacy of scale and detail evokes the rich feel which abstract versions of Persian miniatures and even medieval illuminations would have, if such things existed. *Washington Post* critic Michael Welzenbach called them...*little gems...executed with the same finesse as his larger works...but freer and less rigidly constructed.*[30] By 1992, the BR Kornblatt Gallery had closed and de Looper was now showing his large paintings as well as his small work at the Jones Troyer Fitzpatrick Gallery. When Welzenbach reviewed de Looper's 1992 exhibition there, he noted that the freedom and improvisatory qualities of the small works were now also visible in de Looper's new large paintings: *Jagged white lines and nervous squiggles of vivid orange or red dance on the picture's surfaces. There are neon-intense bolts of color traversing muted, overlapping transparencies of pale earth green and brown, and swaths of bright pigment breaking through cages of sharply drawn straight black lines.*[31]

The artist had reached a stage in his development in which he could confidently shift from one influence to another and combine multiple influences at will to create successful paintings, as clearly evidenced in this 1992 exhibition and those of the next few years. For example, there were two series of small works shown in 1992, *Tesuque Paintings* and *Native Colors*. Their titles are references to the Southwest, especially Santa Fe and Taos, New Mexico, where de Looper has been vacationing for many years.

In reviewing the exhibition for *ARTnews*, Jean Lawlor Cohen described the *Tesuque Paintings* as predominantly black and silver in which their...*outline 'accents' detach themselves. They hover like retinal floaters at some distance from the canvas edge, in tense competition with flattened geometric forms either painted bright green or submerged in blackness.*[32]

One work from the *Native Colors* series has a black triangle wedged between fields of green with a red-orange squiggle on the lower right. This squiggle, rather calligraphic in nature, is complemented by five similar markings in white spread along the top of the canvas.

Although the direct inspiration for the overall painting is the American Southwest, the calligraphic quality of the squiggles derives from Asian sources. Such mixing of influences is not unusual in de Looper's work from the nineties. This is clear from large works like *Black Mesa* of 1992 (Fig. 15) and *Indian Dancer* of 1991 which were shown along with the *Tesuque* and *Native Colors* series. In *Black Mesa*, named for a land form near Santa Fe, the artist has introduced on a textured black field a notched rectangle of copper placed at an angle to the bottom of the picture. With its colored forms cropped by the edges of the canvas, this painting has the compositional structure and tension of a typical John Marin Cubist-inspired landscape of Maine painted in the twenties. Again this is not surprising for an exhibition of Marin's work was one of the first shows that de Looper had seen at The Phillips decades before.

A variety of approaches and influences can also be seen in his 1993 exhibition at the Troyer Fitzpatrick Lassman Gallery. For example, *Ju-Ju* of 1993 (NIE), has a more geometric structure with its central rectangle of drab green held in place on a red-orange field by tabs of orange at the top, and tabs of black at the bottom; this Peter Halley-like compositional format is subtly transformed by the addition of two parallel calligraphic lines in black across the upper tab. Here Eastern calligraphy meets Western geometry, something the likes of which occurs in his 1995 exhibition at Troyer Fitzpatrick Lassman in works such as *East West Encounter* mentioned above.

The most recent phase of the de Looper's work is, in some ways, his richest. The confluence of influences from his small works, from the prints and handmade paper works he has been producing at Pyramid Atlantic, and from his earlier work, has fed an inventive mind. A rich stream of art has resulted. The level of activity and quality of work is truly amazing, yet it still relies on color as an expressive vehicle in the creation of beauty. In a recent letter, de Looper wrote that: *Since I am a colorist, my art means to me color, texture, and composition. Used successfully, these three components are important in my paintings to convey the message of 'beauty.'*[33]

The "message of 'beauty,'" however, is difficult to convey; and yet it is somehow fundamental to human existence. The decorative patterns and color of the earliest utilitarian objects of many cultures are an attempt to make such objects special, to remove them from the drudgery of ordinary existence. From this impulse, painting as a fine art derives, moving from the surface of objects to the surface of walls for better contemplation and appreciation.

The need to delight the eye and mind in order to feel truly alive is the "message of 'beauty'." That this need begins in our long-forgotten past testifies to its importance as a fundamental aspect of our very being. In continuing this search for beauty, Willem de Looper reaffirms a fundamental aspect of our humanity, and it is in this spirit that this retrospective exhibition celebrates his art.

Howard Risatti
May 1996

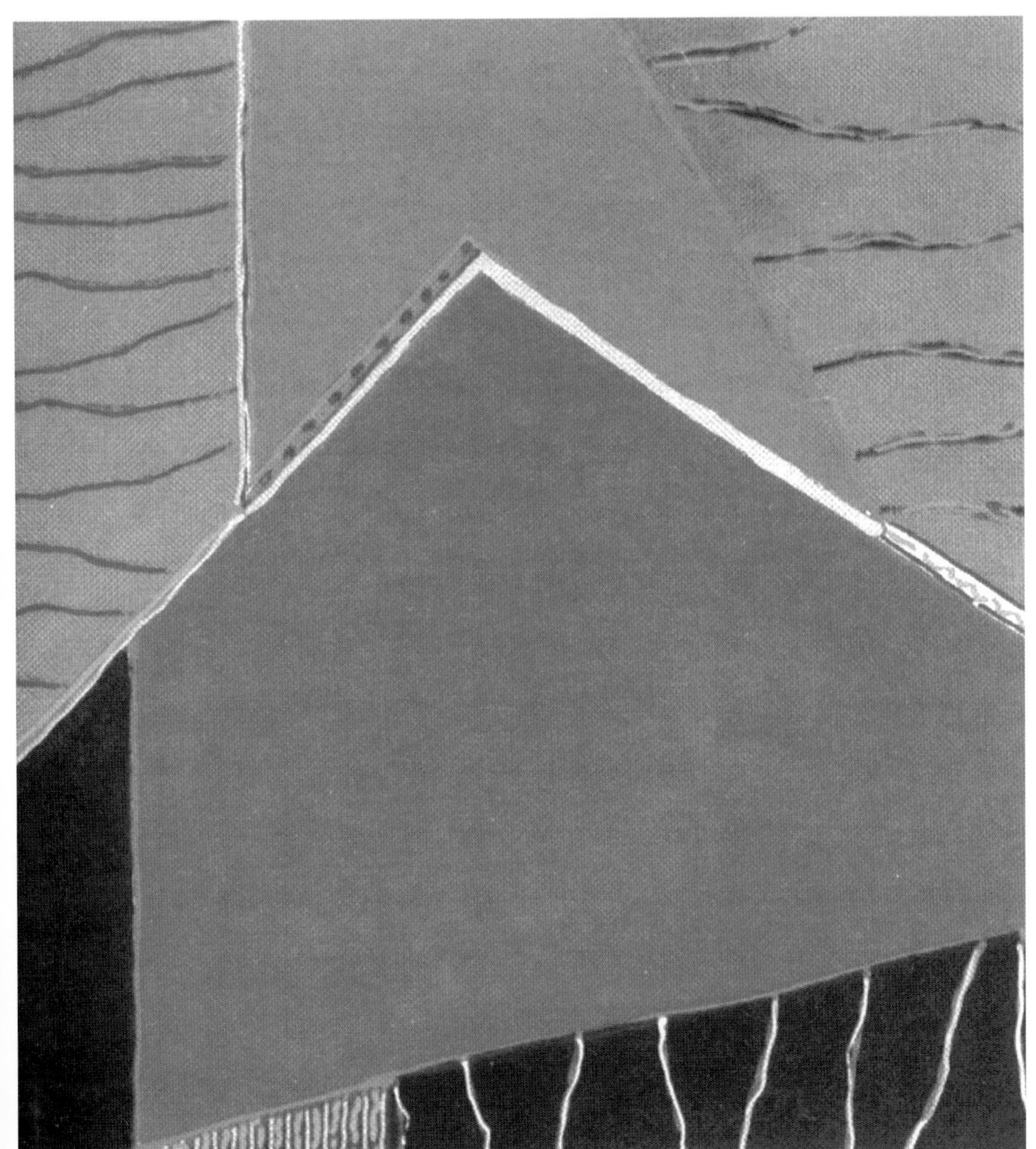

Untitled, 1985
68" x 60"
acrylic on canvas
Collection of the artist
Figure 17

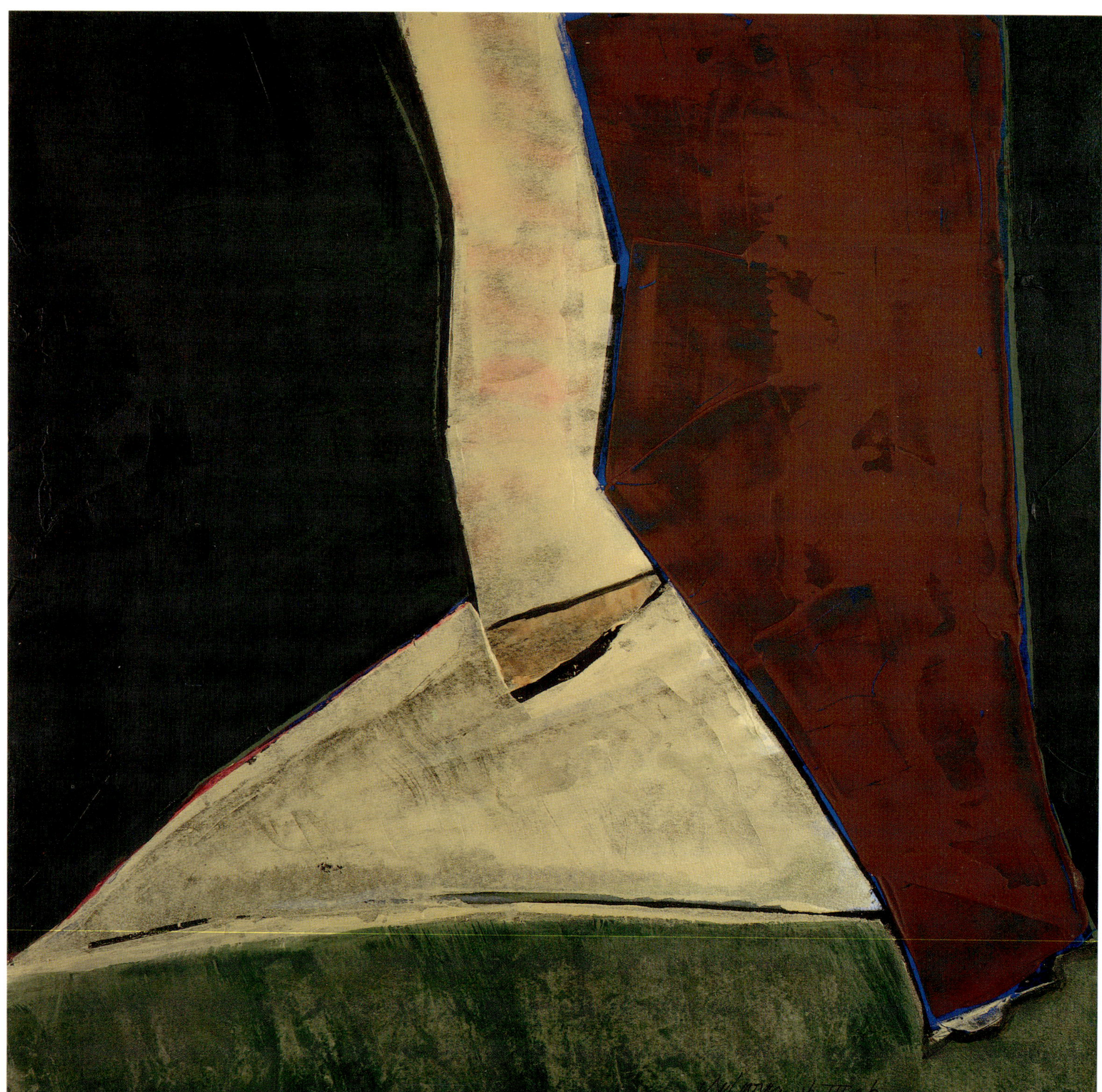

Untitled, 1996
18" x 18"
acrylic on canvas
Collection of the artist
Figure 18

[1] I would like to thank my former student Diane Biddle for assisting me in researching aspects of Willem de Looper's background for this essay. The reader should also recognize the biographical chronology in this catalogue.

[2] Previously, de Looper had also attended the *John Marin Memorial Exhibition* organized by the Art Galleries at UCLA with a catalogue forward by Duncan Phillips. This exhibition was on view at The Phillips Collection from May 15 to June 30, 1955.

[3] This information appeared in an interview de Looper had with David Schaff, *Art International* (December 1977), 6. The exhibition *Arshile Gorky, 1904-1948* was organized by the Museum of Modern Art in New York; it was on view at the Washington Gallery of Modern Art from March 12 to April 14, 1963.

[4] It was the work of these artists which he saw at the World's Fair that convinced him to become an artist instead of an illustrator. Just before he was drafted into the army, he was prepared to take a job at Kahn's Department Store in advertising doing layouts and illustrations.

[5] Up to the mid-1960s, de Looper painted in a variety of styles trying to develop his own "voice." The works of Arthur Dove, in their quality of abstraction from nature, are an important influence on him in these years. Dove, of course, is amply represented in The Phillips Collection since Duncan Phillips was one of Dove's principal patrons for many years.

[6] Clement Greenberg, *"Avant-garde and Kitsch,"* 1939, but reprinted in *Art and Culture (Boston: Beacon Press; 1961), 6.*

[7] Richard Serra's works from the sixties are typical of Process Art. Such works emphasize the central importance of the "action" or "verb form" (pouring, throwing, stacking, leaning) used to make the piece. In the case of Louis, the idea of pouring as a central compositional device begun in the fifties. In the 1960s, with the *Unfurled* series, the process takes on a more predetermined quality in the way paint is poured across opposing corners of the canvas for mirrored compositional affects. And just before his death in 1962, Louis's pouring becomes even more pre-determined as it forms precise geometric compositions of variously colored stripes.

[8] Benjamin Forgey, "The Question is…To Paint, or Not…," *The Sunday Star* (September 15, 1968). De Looper also made a point of the differences between his work and Gilliam's in his *Art International* with David Schaff, op.cit., 48).

[9] Benjamin Forgey, *"De Looper: Artist Without a Niche," Evening Star (November 10, 1970).*

[10] David Schaff, op.cit., 49.

[11] Willem de Looper, unpublished interview with Cynthia J. McCabe, Washington, D.C., September 1975. Cited in *The Golden Door: Artist-Immigrants of America, 1876-1976,* exhibition catalogue, (Washington, D.C.: Hirshhorn Museum and Sculpture Garden; 1976), 372. De Looper spoke fluent English before he came to America and read and copied illustrations out of American magazines. *(The Saturday Evening Post, Colliers, The New Yorker);* he also used the USIA Library. His brother Hans, who had a Ph.D and was in the Dutch Foreign Service, sent him copies of *Li'l Abner* by Al Capp and the works of Bill Malden which he also copied. His inter-

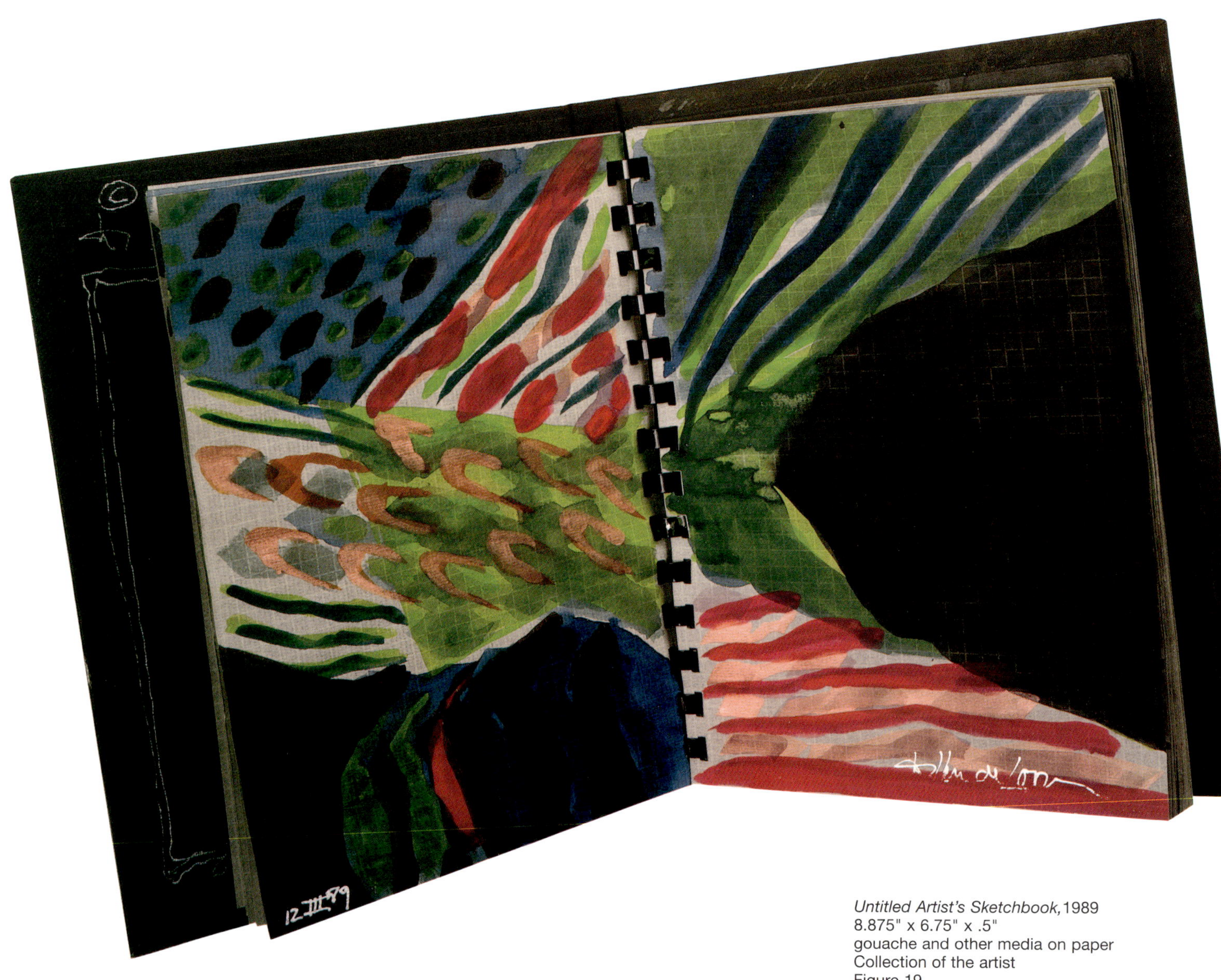

Untitled Artist's Sketchbook, 1989
8.875" x 6.75" x .5"
gouache and other media on paper
Collection of the artist
Figure 19

est in jazz was cultivated while listening to Armed Forces Network and the BBC; his favorite musicians were Benny Goodman, Charlie Parker, Errol Gardner, and Dizzy Gillespie.

[12] Ray Kass, "The Paintings of Willem de Looper; 1973-1976," Kornblatt Gallery exhibition essay, from October 24 through December 1, 1983.

[13] Barbara Novak, *American Painting of the Nineteenth Century* (New York: Praeger Publishers; 1969), 18.

[14] Barbara Novak, op.cit., 122.

[15] James Mahoney, "Willem de Looper at BR Kornblatt," *Art in America* (February 1988), 150-51.

[16] Willem de Looper letter to Anna B. Frances, October 1995. Archives of the artist. At American University, de Looper was disc jockey on the AU station specializing in jazz.

[17] Cynthia Saltzman, "Willem de Looper," *ARTnews* (December 1979), p. 170. The exhibition ran from September 14 through October 14, 1979.

[18] Ibid.

[19] Jane Addams Allen, "Galleries/Willem de Looper," *The Washington Times* (November 3, 1983).

[20] De Looper suggested that these curved lines may be influenced by the arches of the Islamic architecture of Tashkent and Samarkand which he saw in 1977. Conversation with the author.

[21] De Looper said he originally thought of calling the painting *"Tunisia on My Mind,"* but felt the Gillespie reference would be too strong. So, he settled for "*Tunis*." Conversation with the author.

[22] The exhibition *Morris Graves: Vision of the Inner Eye* (catalogue by Kass with introduction by Theodore Wolff) remained at The Phillips Collection from April 9 to May 29, 1983. It subsequently traveled to the Greenville County Museum in South Carolina; the Whitney Museum of American Art in New York; The Oakland Museum in California; the Seattle Museum of Art in Washington; and the San Diego Museum of Art in California.

[23] Benjamin Forgey, "Willem de Looper at Kornblatt," *The Washington Post* (November 10, 1983).

[24] The chronology of influences on this work is somewhat difficult to unravel. De Looper's notebook dates the 3-week Japan trip to September 30, 1983. At the beginning of November of that year he had an exhibition of new works on paper at the Kornblatt Gallery. Already in a review of these works, Benjamin Forgey comments on de Looper's use of "painted lines," "brilliant hues," and "metallic colors" as quite a shift. It seems improbable that de Looper could have painted the works for this show in the last week of October after returning from Japan. For this reason, the use of metallic colors and the new compositional format is probably not a direct result of the Japan trip. Influence from this trip probably does surface in the use of black and the "screen" formats in later works.

[25] Other shows he curated were the *Washington Print* and the *Guillermo Roux* exhibitions in 1988. He also curated the *Howard Ben Tre/William Willis* exhibition in 1989.

[26] The Shippee Gallery exhibition ran from February 18 through March 19, 1988.

[27] The inspiration for the shape of this copper curve actually comes from a nearby curved roof vent visible from the artist's studio window.

[28] The Kornblatt Gallery exhibition, which ran from February 25 through March 25, overlapped an exhibition of his "book works" held at the Jones Troyer Fitzpatrick Gallery from March 2 to April 22, 1989.

[29] Because Nara was the Japanese capital from 710-794, it has many Buddhist monuments. Today it still contains many of Japan's most significant cultural sites including the five-story pagoda and complex of buildings at Horyuji temple, supposedly the oldest wood structure in the world. It also has the largest bronze statue of Buddha in Asia (about 50 feet high) and a famous statue made in the dry lacquer technique imported into Japan from China.

[30] Michael Welzenbach, "Paint for Paint's Sake," *The Washington Post* (March 4, 1989), C2.

[31] Michael Welzenbach, "For de Looper, A Change of Color," *The Washington Post* (January 11, 1992), G2.

[32] Jean Lawlor Cohen, "Willem de Looper," *ARTnews* (summer 1992), 144-45.

[33] Letter to Anna B. Frances (October 1995). Archives of the artist.

A style of his own

Willem is my friend and sometimes travel partner. I learned from these experiences that his paintings are not abstractions of nature, but visualizations of his response to nature. He has fully explored and exploited the surface and stage of canvas and paper. De Looper developed a style of his own in the bastion of abstract and color field painting. The mark-making and edges of his colors are polymorphous in their references to places he loves, such as New Mexico.

I am grateful that he continues to carry the banner for abstract painting in this city.

Manfred Baumgartner
Baumgartner Galleries, Inc.
Washington, D.C.

The artist's notebooks

In 1989, Washingtonians were able for the first time to enjoy another important aspect of Willem de Looper's art. When we asked Mr. de Looper if he had small works appropriate for the small space of the then Jones Troyer Fitzpatrick Gallery, we were surprised to learn of the existence of the notebooks. What a thrill it was to discover in his studio a treasure trove of small accomplished paintings on the pages of beautifully decorated books. Each book was a different size and shape, many with spiral bindings, all filled with amazing watercolors. Every painting was carefully signed and dated and a few bore the name of the place where they were made. There appeared to be a painting for each day and one or more books from each of the past 25 years.

The notebooks were the journals of a life in art, the life of a traveling curator, and the life of an imaginative and disciplined painter. What the books were not were sketchbooks, for page after page revealed perfectly realized paintings. Only occasionally one found a drawing, but always a drawing in color and never a partial idea. These were the ideas and experiments that might appear later in larger works, but there were no sketches to be later enlarged.

After the pleasure of discovery came the problem of how to exhibit the book works properly. Mr. de Looper allowed a few pages to be excised from books dating from the mid-seventies through the eighties, always protecting the integrity of the original journal. However, one book, "The Italian Book," was completely unbound. The pages of this book were of strangely colored construction paper, and it was informative to see the ways in which a great colorist could turn to advantage the brown, pink, and lavender pages as the foundation of his many layered images. The exhibition of pages from a whole book also revealed the unfailing quality from page to page of each entry. No pages were torn out or pasted over. Instead, as in his large works, corrections to forms or line were made by over painting with watercolor or gouache.

One of the many lessons about Mr. de Looper's work revealed by a study of the book works was his uncanny ability to experiment and change in the course of a painting and to achieve new lively shapes within a small space. The qualities of elegant geometry, unexpected color harmonies, and provocative lines—characteristics of his canvases—were all present. The sense of perfectly balanced forms was also apparent. We know that he worked on his canvases on the floor of his studio walking around them as he painted with brush or roller, and we sensed that he turned the books around as he worked at a desk in his hotel room or studio. The detailed gem-like paintings were not casually made, but refined and completed with great care.

Despite the similarities with larger paintings of the same years, however, there was in the books a unique feeling of freedom, spontaneity, and playfulness. They were also very personal journals and the fanciful flight of one day might well by followed by a somber mood the next. The books have been compared by critics to illuminated manuscripts, perhaps because of Mr. de Looper's consistent use of gold and other metallic paints, and because of his penchant for saturated red, and the familiar medieval blue. The effect of the book pages, however, seems quite different. The only narrative they illustrate is the important one of Mr. de Looper's development as an artist.

The small works were much admired. They deepened an appreciation of de Looper's skills as a painter of color and form and they pointed toward new works to come. Book works were exhibited with larger paintings in 1992 and 1993 and it seemed clear that the new works on canvas showed increasing elements of spontaneity and experimentation. In an interview in 1979, Mr. de Looper said that he had let his early interest in drawing be overcome by his care for color. In both small and large paintings of the eighties and nineties, drawing reemerged as an important element in his compositions. The elusive lines which could encase a form or float free of it, were increasingly complex. The layers of underpainting could best be seen where lines disappeared and then reappeared in the shimmering color combinations. Another aspect of the book pages, the varied textures created in watercolor, also began increasingly to enrich the canvases. Other elements of the book works—the influences of Southwestern and Japanese motifs, the illusion of symmetry, the mountain and window forms, the daring use of black and bright metallics—invigorated the work on panel and canvas.

Two very important exhibitions in the mid-nineties further illuminated de Looper's mastery of small format painting. In the 1995 exhibition at the Troyer Fitzpatrick Lassman Gallery, the small works emphasized Mr. de Looper's ever bolder use of blacks. Using a spiral notebook of large black paper, he relied heavily on the effects of black on black, and shining metallic blues, silvers, and bronze on black. There were in this book, more frequent references to the Japanese culture with the use of the kimono and fan shapes and heavily reliance upon a lacquer red. The black-page book was an illustration of Mr. de Looper's continued ability to achieve new effects. Many of the nineties books, unlike the earlier journals, have been created with the knowledge that they would be exhibited. Now the pages are almost always covered with acrylic paint, although occasional works in pastel and gouache are found. In 1996, The Phillips Collection mounted a retrospective exhibition of framed book pages. Like the 1989 exhibition, it was a revelation but now to a much wider audience. This beautiful exhibition illustrated again Mr. de Looper's infinite variety of imaginative forms, his dedication to subtle color harmonies, and his unerring ability to make large and complex paintings on his small book pages.

Sally Troyer
Troyer Fitzpatrick Lassman Gallery
Washington, D.C.

An abstract working space

Some painters, including myself, do not care what chair they are sitting on. It does not even have to be a comfortable one…Rather they have found that painting to be painting at all, in fact is a way of living today, a style of living, so to speak. That is where the form of it lies. It is exactly in its uselessness that it is free. Those artists do not want to conform. They only want to be inspired.

Willem de Kooning
1951 MOMA Symposium:
"What Abstract Art Means To Me"

Many more years ago than I care to count, Willem de Looper visited the studio I was moving into above what became the Fraser's Stable gallery behind S Street in Washington, D.C. After carefully surveying the space and the unpacked boxes, he turned back to me and said, *There's no going back, you know.* There had been and would be other addresses but I knew he wasn't talking about the physical space. He was commenting on a way of living and the establishment of a more abstract working space, not confined by the size of a room. At this point I was working at The Phillips Collection, had an MFA, and had exhibited my work. But this comment, coming from Willem, meant to me that for the first time I had received credentials as a painter. This statement was delivered, however, not as a compliment but as a challenge.

The physical size of Willem's studio is surprisingly small considering the scale and volume of the art produced there. But the working space he has established is vast and dynamic. When on various occasions I have helped Willem transport work from his studio to an exhibition, I have felt like we were performing the circus act where far too many clowns come out of a tiny car. What is critical to his work though is not the size of the studio but the fact that it is literally and figuratively where he lives. The rooms that are not used for actually painting provide interesting insight into the context in which he does paint. Upon entering Willem and Frauke's apartment one sees: most prominently, a display of art of catholic taste, from African sculpture to Pat Steir; a collection of music on records, tapes and discs that rivals most shops; shelves filled with books on an array of subjects; and an extremely comfortable sitting area that has accommodated an amazing series of guests from all stations in life.

The rooms that provide the working studio are incredibly well organized and function in such a way that he can seamlessly integrate the work of making art into the myriad activities that comprise anyone's everyday life. There is separate space with a drawing table for the works on paper and the notebooks, and a room for the paintings where there are only the works in progress and the materials necessary for them.

Pieces of this physical studio travel with him wherever he goes in the form of notebooks of many shapes and sizes, their pages filled with everything from small works in paint to experiments with almost anything that can leave a mark. Within Not simply small studies for paintings these notebooks there are many surprises. Not simply small studies for paintings but works that stand on their own and reveal many avenues of exploration, even including very direct drawings of figures and interiors in a variety of media. They may become things that are exhibited as "artists' books" but before they leave Willem's hands they are simply studio space. Postcards with photographs or reproductions and old announcements have also frequently provided unusual underpaintings for a kind of visual play. This experimentation is not limited to two dimensions. While the paintings and notebooks are what Willem is best known for, he has also transformed everyday objects with paint. Little boxes, small objects and even small tables have become vehicles that have carried his painterliness and color into three dimensions.

This way of living has provided an environment where the process of making art so totally and naturally permeates Willem's life that the idea of "working" or "making art" as a separate occupation is an alien concept. Even Willem's salaried "job" (his career at The Phillips Collection) was in a place devoted to integrating great art into a home-like atmosphere rather than isolating it in the traditional museum environment.

Keats wrote, *That if Poetry comes not as naturally as the Leaves to a tree it had better not come at all.* That certainly does not mean that art is produced without labor (Keats also said in the same letter that it is *easier to think what Poetry should be than to write it*) but that it should be a natural procedure, not a contrived academic exercise or the routine skilled labor necessary for the production of objects. (The artist Yuri Schwebler once said, *If I wanted to make expensive objects I'd make Mercedes-Benz.*) The making of art is for Willem exactly this kind of natural process and is far removed from the kind of wider interest and scrutiny brought by any exhibition, much less an exhibition of this scope. This environment is one that over the years provides a place for private experimentation and incremental growth and change. That is where the form of it lies.

There was a reception given in Willem's honor in the Music Room of The Phillips Collection when he left his full-time position there. In his remarks at that time he mentioned that it was appropriate that the sculpture garden was being dismantled at the same time (to make way for the remodeling of 1612 21st Street into the Goh Annex) since he had arrived when the sculpture garden first opened. He then said, *Although there was never a cafe in that garden, there was a period when it was known for the best lunches in Washington.* He was referring to the countless brown bag lunches taken outside with others who worked at The Phillips (mostly artists), those who would occasionally join us (local and visiting artists), and the remarkable conversations which ensued. It is in conversation with Willem that one can best appreciate the extensive frame of reference that defines Willem's working space. While his conversation at some point always seems to return to painting, the painter discussed could just as easily be Puvis de Chavannes as Robert Ryman, Cezanne, or someone obscure whose work he had seen just once somewhere. He can talk passionately about music, especially the jazz he knows so intimately. Current world events also play a large part, whether from the front page or a small story from the *New York Times* Metro section. Lest this sound too serious, it should also be said that laughter plays an important role in the rhythm of these conversations and the NBA can easily replace art during the playoffs.

There is, I believe, a similar conversational give and take manner in the way Willem actually paints. There is an intimate, intense relationship with the work in progress. He "listens" intently to the materials for new ideas and responds appropriately, pushing and challenging, exploring the subject at hand. This is when Willem uses his warehouse of a working space to find visual counterparts for the complexity of experience as nuance of light and dark, shape and line, edge, surface and color. This intense kind of dialogue with the materials gives each individual painting an integrity that prevents it from ever being merely the product of a skilled hand. Each painting has its own history and presence and like Willem's conversation, can be light-hearted or serious, frivolous or profound, intellectual or sensual or, as some of the best of them are, many of these things at the same time. All of them, I believe, echo the rhythms of daily living and are always beautiful in that, even at their most somber, they are an affirmation of life and its sensations.

Wilfred Brunner
Artist and Teacher
Takoma Park, MD

And surely you have seen, in the darkness of the innermost rooms of these huge buildings to which sunlight never penetrates, how the gold leaf of a sliding door or screen will pick up a distant glimmer from the garden, then suddenly send forth an ethereal glow, a faint golden cast into the enveloping darkness, like a glow upon the horizon at sunset.

Jun'ichiro Tanizaki,
In Praise of Shadows

Tanizaki encapsulates that quintessential beauty of Japan. His descriptions are especially evocative concerning the mysterious effects of light and shadow on mood. There is similar poetry in de Looper's art. In the presence of his art, we enter a spiritual place that is a synthesis of the many visual responses that have formed de Looper's aesthetic.

An appreciation for the Japanese aesthetic is particularly strong in his work from the late eighties and early nineties. De Looper has visited Japan twice: once in 1977, then for three weeks in 1983. The influence of these trips can be sensed in a penchant for using textured gold and red motifs against black ground, reading like smooth lacquerware; subtle monochromatic papers and printed colors with applied gold leaf accents; and architectonic shapes which remind one of the angular stiffness of ritual clothing, ceremonial entrances, and mountain shrines. The rich black of Japanese brush painting and diptych formats are recalled. Sometimes, painting surfaces have a raked appearance, suggestive of textures in contemplative gardens. The Japanese shoji screen shape and the wooden stretcher bars of the canvas are echoed in some paintings. The artist has even painted on the backs of stretchers. In looking at the paintings, we can almost hear the sound of dark wooden screens opening and closing quietly in hushed rooms. His best works achieve a monumental grandeur akin to the aesthetic appreciation of an elegant structure in modern architecture.

His paintings and works on paper are rich in color and solidly composed. Color and form interlock, balanced on the picture plane, revealing the edges of planes, where one color slides coolly against another, creating linear boundaries. The artist thus creates an architectural sense of space with planes that appear cantilevered. Utilization of metallic paint in some works introduces a minimal, sculptural element that again relates to architecture and design.

His smaller acrylic works on paper represent a personal form of observation, done in different locales in the course of his travels. They effectively record the artist's responses, utilizing abstract symbols, in notations that might later be translated to a larger format. The artist's love of drawing is evident. These are inspired works in their own right with a strong graphic design sensitivity. Both formal and playful, somber and characterized by humor, they thrive on the push and pull of intense color in small, book-like formats. In recent years, de Looper has expanded his repertoire with monotypes and hand papermaking. The experience of working at Pyramid Atlantic has been liberating. There, improvisational techniques and forms can lead to "happy" accidents. Working with printers realized a new form of expression. The process of painting with pulp paper squeezed out of a plastic receptacle, just as in some painting color squeezed from a tube, is used to make lines or shapes, entertained new expressions. The paper pulp medium, in which the formed paper and pigment become one substance, refers back to the direct experience of structuring pure color so characteristic of the Washington Color School. A spontaneous approach to painting is nurtured in this environment, where there is also a sense of discovery and play at work in the print studio much different from the isolation of the private studio. An admirer of Minimalism as well as Diebenkorn and Kandinsky, de Looper's expressive use of painterly abstraction emerges as a signature element in a style that is capable of endless innovation.

Lenore D. Miller
Director,
The George Washington University Dimock Gallery
Washington, D.C.

An artist's artist

For more than twenty years I have admired Willem de Looper's dedication to his own strong, central, abstract vision. Although he has explored and made good use of many variations in style, medium, palette, and technique, he has always worked within the bounds of this personal vision. And though he is keenly interested in the styles of other artists, past and present, his own paintings and drawings invariably have an unmistakable character of their own.

I also greatly admire Willem's absolute dedication to the hard work of painting and drawing. Year after year, in good times and bad, he has produced a large body of work. His sketchbooks have always been near at hand for recording daytime inspirations, and I know that even after a long day's work as curator of The Phillips Collection, he regularly painted late into the night.

Willem is an artist's artist, steadily producing the beautiful product of his personal vision. Washington is richer for his presence.

Laughlin Phillips
Chairman,
The Phillips Collection
Washington, D.C.

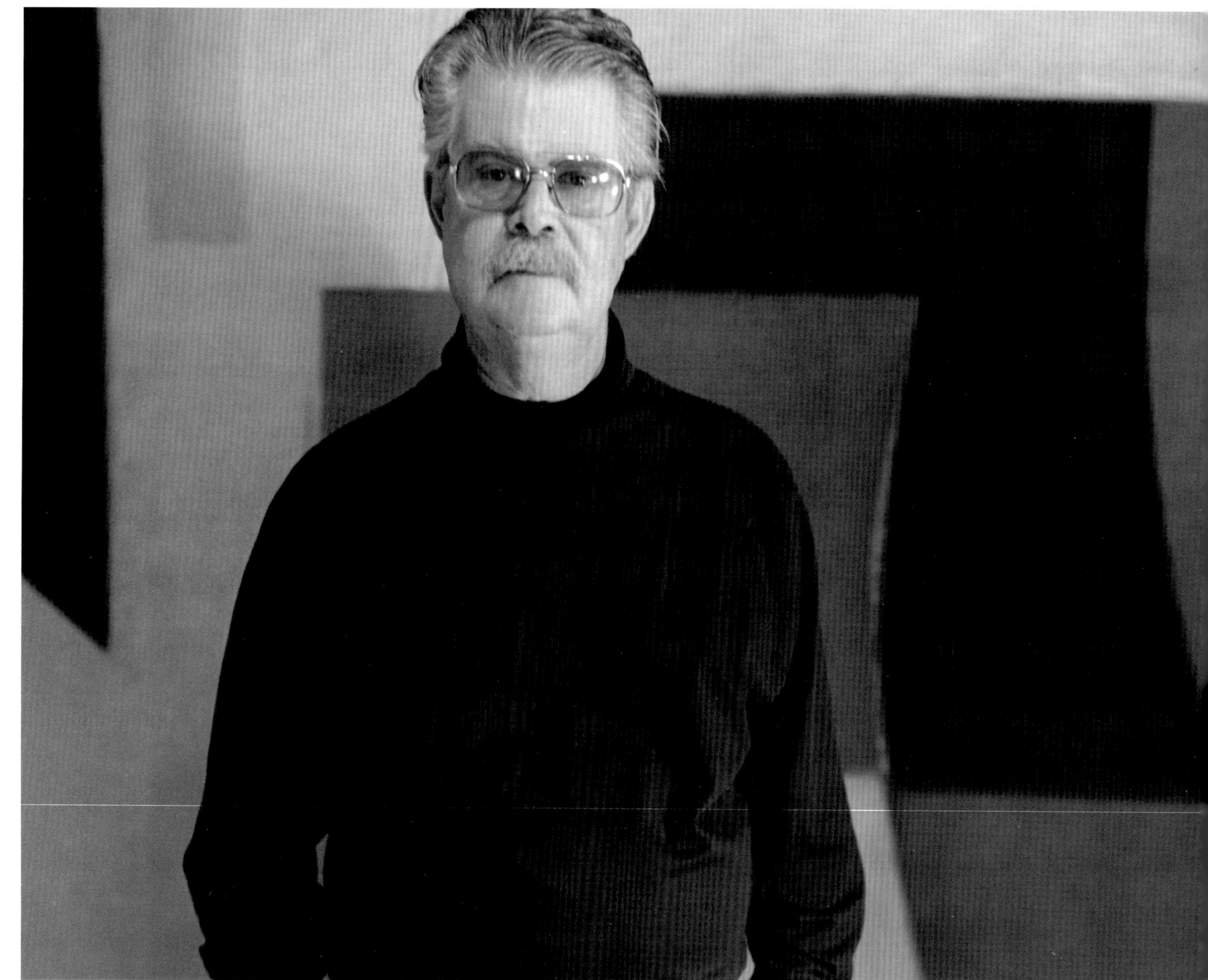

Chronology of the artist

Historical context

1932-1945

Willem de Looper was born October 30, 1932, the third child of Wilhelmina Johanna and Henri Bastiaan de Looper in The Hague, the Netherlands. As a young child, Willem attended a Montessori school. These schools were emerging at the time as a revolutionary approach to early childhood education. The Montessori system placed equal emphasis on imaginative and cognitive development; children worked with shapes and color at the same time that they were taught language and mathematical concepts.

By the time de Looper was seven years old, Germany had invaded Poland and World War II had begun. Very shortly thereafter, the Netherlands came under German occupation. De Looper's father was a partner in a small bank in a neighborhood where the Nazi headquarters were located. De Looper recalls that, during the War, the family moved three times within The Hague as the Nazi occupiers shifted the city's population to counteract the development of cells of resistance.

After one of these moves, they lived with a friend and client of de Looper's father who was an excellent pianist. During the wartime occupation, movement was severely restricted (one had to have a pass to leave one's neighborhood), and cultural life had all but disappeared (museums were closed during the War). In this constricted environment, music provided solace and stimulation. De Looper attributes his lifelong passion for music–which has profoundly affected his creative life to the present–to this experience.

The 1930s were momentous for art and society in both Europe and the United States. By 1933 important practitioners of bold abstract art had emigrated to the U.S. to escape the threat of Nazism; Hans Hoffman had opened a school in New York, and in the following year another in Provincetown. Hoffman's influence was profound. Clement Greenberg and Harold Rosenberg attended lectures at his New York school in the late thirties, and some of his well-known students included Lee Krasner, Helen Frankenthaler, and Larry Rivers.

Josef Albers left the German Bauhaus and arrived in the U.S. in 1933, the same year Hitler became Chancellor of Germany. Albers taught many important American abstract artists at the Black Mountain School and later at Yale. Among Albers' students was Kenneth Noland, one of the pioneers of what Clement Greenberg later called "post-painterly abstraction" and a founder of the Washington Color School. Many other avant-garde European artists emigrated to the U.S. as World War II got underway. Some settled in Chicago to start the New Bauhaus and others pursued their careers in New York and elsewhere, contributing to American abstraction's ascendance to world prominence.

In the mid-thirties, coinciding with Franklin D. Roosevelt's landslide victory, the U.S. government established the Works Progress Administration (WPA) and the Federal Art Project (FAP), the most well-known of seven separate federal arts programs which employed artists during the Depression. Duncan Phillips was appointed Regional Director of the WPA. Phillips was already an important figure in the art world because of his involvement during World War I in organizing artists to produce

Willen de Looper in his California Street studio in Northwest Washington, D.C.

De Looper drawing at a table at his Montessori school

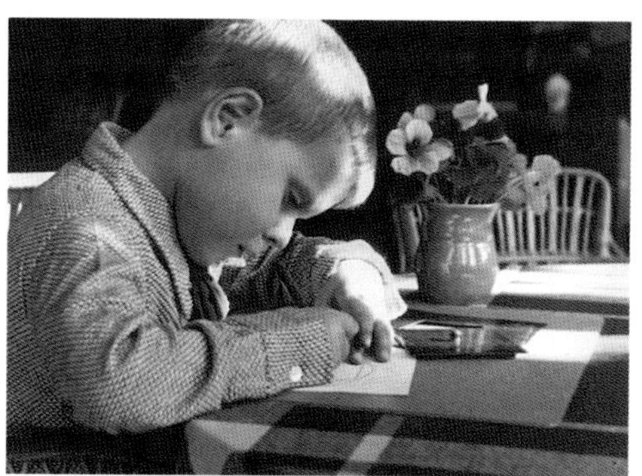

savings bonds and other War support artwork, and because of his establishment of the first American museum of modern art in 1918 on the top two floors of his family's Washington, D.C. mansion. The museum, initially called The Phillips Memorial Gallery, was started by Duncan Phillips as a memorial to his father and brother. The Phillips became home to major works of European Impressionism as well as important collections of first-wave American abstraction: paintings by Arthur Dove, John Marin, Georgia O'Keeffe, and Marsden Hartley, which later had a significant impact on de Looper.

Just as Duncan Phillips was involved in what seem to be opposite camps in twentieth century art, modernism and social realism, so were many other prominent American artists and arts patrons. Although the vast majority of the WPA and other federally-sponsored art fell into the social realist genre, there were significant abstract works produced, as well. Not only was the Mural Section of the Federal Art Project directed by the prominent abstract painter Burgoyne Diller, but several artists who later became leading figures in American Abstract-Expressionism were employed in this program: Rosalind Bengelsdorf (who founded the American Abstract Artists's Association), Ilya Bolotowski, Stuart Davis, Willem de Kooning, Arshile Gorky, and Philip Guston. In addition, Jackson Pollock (whose early work, incidentally, resembled that of regionalist painter Thomas Hart Benton) and Ad Reinhardt, both known for their purely abstract painting, were employed by the Easel Division of the FAP.

In 1935, the new Whitney Museum of American Art in New York sponsored the first exhibition of American abstract *painting, with a catalogue introduction by Stuart Davis.*

In Washington, a school of painting associated with the Phillips Gallery was established in 1930. C. Law Watkins, a Yale classmate and lifelong friend of Duncan Phillips, was Associate Director of the Phillips Gallery and director of this school. From 1932 to 1938, when the school was closed because of the Great Depression, Watkins operated Studio House which combined the functions of a school and a commercial gallery.

In 1942 this Phillips-associated school which had reopened on the top floor of the museum, became part of American University where it soon offered both a B.F.A. and an M.F.A. in painting. The connection with the Phillips was still quite close as students painted and drew at the Gallery several mornings a week. In 1945 with the death of Watkins, the direct affiliation terminated. William Calfee, who had served as a teaching assistant to Watkins at the Phillips Gallery School, became chair of the American University art department in 1946, and Sarah Baker and Robert Gates, both of whom had been associated with the school, became faculty.

During the forties Piet Mondrian arrived in New York, and by 1949, abstraction was well-established, recognized as an artistic vernacular, and hailed as peculiarly "American," as evidenced by the August 1949 Life Magazine *article "Jackson Pollock: Is he the Greatest American Painter?"*

Willem and Frauke at their wedding reception at Jeffer–son Place Gallery in 1969.

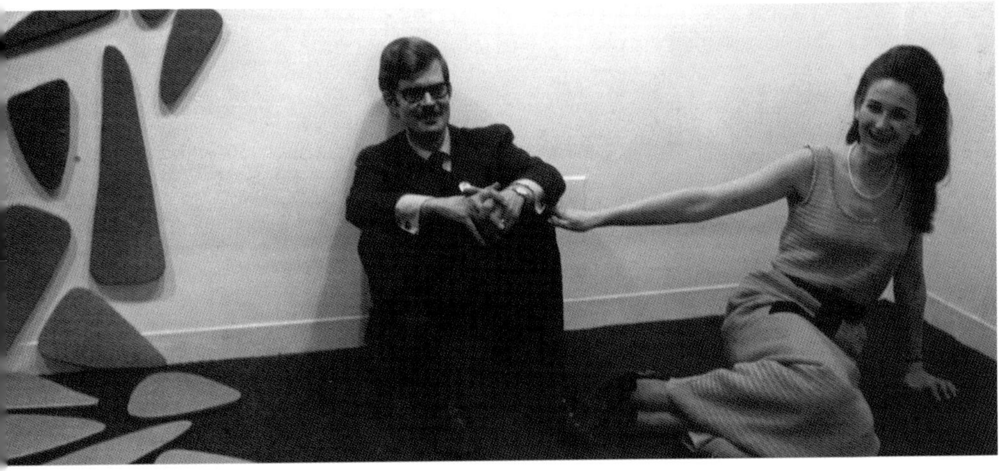

1945-1949

De Looper's interest in drawing became increasingly serious as World War II ended and American publications became available again in the Netherlands. The teenager, who at that point had not yet received formal artistic training, practiced drawing by copying magazine illustrations. De Looper enthusiastically sought out American magazines, especially the *New Yorker*, for its sophisticated drawings and reporting of cultural life in New York. It was from the pages of the *New Yorker* that de Looper began, as he has said, *to build my dreams of a life in the U.S., and of involvement in the music and art world so colorfully depicted in the* New Yorker's *pages.*[1] He was also strongly influenced by the vivid colors and striking graphics, layouts, photography, art, and advertising of the *Saturday Evening Post* and *Life Magazine*. He attributes much of this early access to American publications to his brother, Johan (called Hans) who brought de Looper his first samples of these publications along with books of cartoons by Al Capp and Bill Mauldin, when he returned to the Netherlands from Buenos Aires via New York, after his first posting as a junior diplomat in the Dutch Foreign Service. The influences of these American publications are evident in de Looper's early drawings and watercolors.

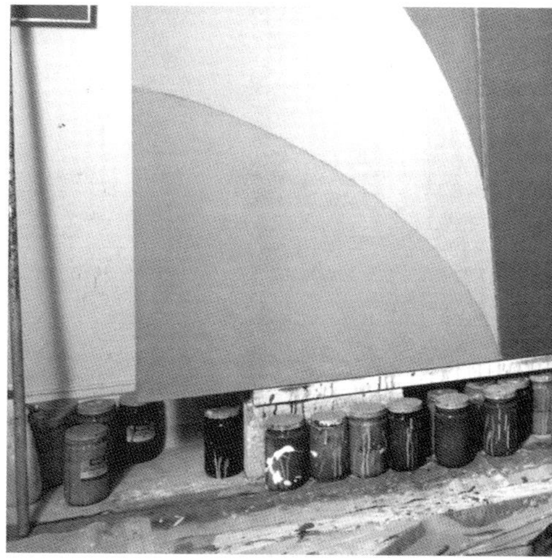

1950-1956

In 1950 at age 17, de Looper joined his 28-year-old brother Hans in Washington, D.C., where he had just begun to work for the International Monetary Fund, the beginning of a 25-year career with that agency. For the first two years Willem was on a tourist visa. By 1953 the family had decided Willem should go to college in the U.S.; he enrolled at American University where he began his first formal study of art with faculty artists Robert Gates, Sarah Baker, and, Ben ("Joe") Summerford who, de Looper says: *was my primary mentor.*[2] He simultaneously majored in economics, a field more acceptable to his family. Willem continued to live with Hans during college and describes his older brother as being like a second father. *I cannot emphasize how much encouragement he gave me to pursue my art. He was always buying me art books. He gave me a Picasso book on the Vollard suite.*

In 1951 the first book about abstract expressionism was published: Abstract Painting: Background and the American Phase, *by Thomas Hess. In the same year* ARTnews *proclaimed that*...a little-known movement is (rapidly changing) into one of growing national importance..., *referring to a diverse group of artists who became the "New York School:" William Basiotes, Robert Motherwell, Barnett Newman, Jackson Pollock, Mark Rothko, Ad Reinhardt, and David Smith.*

The Washington Color School originated with groupings of artists around three institutions in the early 1950s: the American University Art Department where Jack Tworkov, a part-time faculty member, encouraged investigation of the expressive, painterly, gestural mode associated with de Kooning; the Institute of Contemporary Arts, formed in 1947 by Robert Richman to provide classes and exhibit the work of major European and American

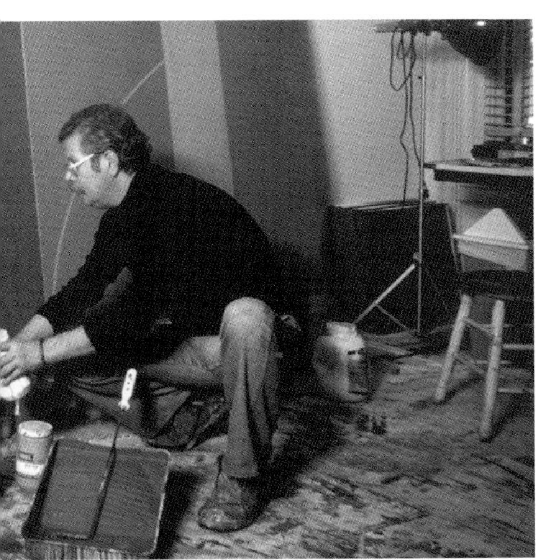

Large painting in process at the Fraser Stable Gallery. De Looper had a one-person exhibition here in 1977.

And, most important, he paid for my education completely. I owe him so much.[3] De Looper soon changed his major to Fine Arts.

While pursuing his undergraduate studies, de Looper organized student shows, served as the art editor of the University's literary journal, and was selected for several local exhibitions featuring outstanding student artists.

He returned frequently to The Hague to visit his mother who had separated from his father and was living opposite the museum which held the largest collection of Piet Mondrian's works. He avidly visited as many newly-opened Dutch art museums as he could during these visits.

contemporary artists; and the Washington Workshop Center for the Arts, organized by Leon and Ida Berkowitz in 1945. The Berkowitzes received support from Elaine and Willem de Kooning for the project, including bringing Washington art to the attention of influential critic Clement Greenberg, who was central to the development of the Washington Color School. He introduced Morris Louis and Kenneth Noland in 1953 (both artists worked in Washington at that time) to the paintings of Pollock and Frankenthaler, and convinced them of his assessment that these two New York artists were the waves of the future for painting. As a direct result, Louis began to create his stained veil paintings in 1954.

1957-1958

In 1957 after graduating from American University with a B.F.A., de Looper began a two-year tour with the U.S. Army in Europe, where he was stationed at Ludwigsburg, near Stuttgart. During this period he began to collect and study major art magazines and journals, and to travel extensively throughout Europe to see the great masterpieces of Western art in major museums. In 1958 the young artist was exposed for the first time to Abstract Expressionist canvases, which he saw at the American Pavilion at the Brussels World's Fair. Throughout his Army tour, de Looper continued to draw and paint in notebooks he carried with him and at the Army base's craft shop. He was married for a brief time to a former school friend from the Netherlands while in the Army.

In 1959 the Museum of Modern Art organized a traveling exhibition, The New American Painting, *which was shown in eight European countries, including Belgium, where it was featured at the U.S. pavilion at the Brussels World's Fair.*

	Chronology of the artist	*Historical context*

1959-1965

Upon returning to Washington in 1959, de Looper continued to be particularly fascinated with the works of Mark Rothko and Barnett Newman, as well as with the work of several artists involved in what would soon be known as the Washington Color School. Abstraction and strong emphasis on color, the qualities of the American Abstract Expressionists' works that had made a deep impression on de Looper in Brussels, continued to interest him during the sixties. He was also strongly attracted to the use of thinned down paint *(I loved the idea of the paint 'disappearing' into the canvas,* he says[4]) like that used by Morris Louis.

In 1959 de Looper was hired as a guard at The Phillips Gallery. The position came through with the help of Doris Woodward who worked at the Gallery and who was at that time married to de Looper's former American University classmate William Woodward. De Looper has noted that during 1962 and1963 he filled a notebook with watercolors that emulated works in The Phillips Collection by Paul Klee, John Marin, and Arthur Dove. Gorky and Louis compositions, available for study in other Washington galleries and museums, were also influential,[5] as were "spiritualist" works of Kandinsky and Arp, though he maintains that he *was not drawn to the theosophist and other quasi-religious underpinnings of these works–I just liked them as art!*[6] De Looper continues to the present to deny "spiritualist" intentions in his own paintings.

During the early 1960s, de Looper experimented with Color School painting processes: spraying, rolling, pouring, and sponging. Color replaced line in the artist's attempts to convey a sense of spaciousness and volume.[7] In 1964 he began to

In 1962 Pop Art made a dramatic debut in New York at the New Realists *show at the Sidney Janis Gallery, signaling what many saw as a return to the object. The show and the artists were roundly denounced by many critics, including Harold Rosenberg. More typical of the time was adherence to the abstract expressionist orthodoxy of critic Michael Fried who, in 1965, pronounced the current work of de Kooning, Frankenthaler, Gorky, Gottlieb, Hoffman, Kline, Louis, Motherwell, Newman, Pollock, Rothko, Smith, and Still…*the best new painting anywhere…and for 20 years or more.

The sixties also saw the rapid development of "minimalist" tendencies among New York artists: another challenge to abstract expressionism and post-painterly abstraction. These tendencies took two somewhat divergent directions: abstraction devoid of decorative detail and emphasizing geometry (Donald Judd, Tony Smith, Sol LeWitt, Robert Ryman, Agnes Martin, and Frank Stella); and presentation of "found" objects and materials as art (Carl Andre, Robert Morris, Robert Rauschenberg, Bruce Nauman, and Eva Hesse).

By the late fifties and early sixties, the Washington Color School was beginning to be recognized as a movement and all of the key figures were living and working in the Washington area. By 1959 Louis (1912-1962) was well-established with his veil-like stain paintings, and Noland (b. 1924) had broken through to his boldly simple geometries in opaque stained color. Louis and Noland are acknowledged as the primary influences in the development of the Washington Color School. Noland taught both Thomas Downing (1928-1985) and Howard Mehring (1931-1978) at Catholic University and through the Workshop, work in Magna (a type of acrylic paint), and later with water-based, acrylic emulsions that allowed him to create the veiled effects of staining that characterized the works in his first major group show at the 1965 *Washington Area Exhibition* sponsored by the Corcoran Gallery of Art. He received an honorable mention in painting at this exhibition for his work titled *October Sheath*.

Other exhibitions in which his work was represented during these years include: a drawing show and the annual exhibition of Washington artists at the Franz Bader Gallery, both in 1961; exhibitions at the Art Society of the International Monetary Fund in 1962 and at the Society of Washington Artists in 1964 and 1965; and a group show at the Jefferson Place Gallery in 1965.

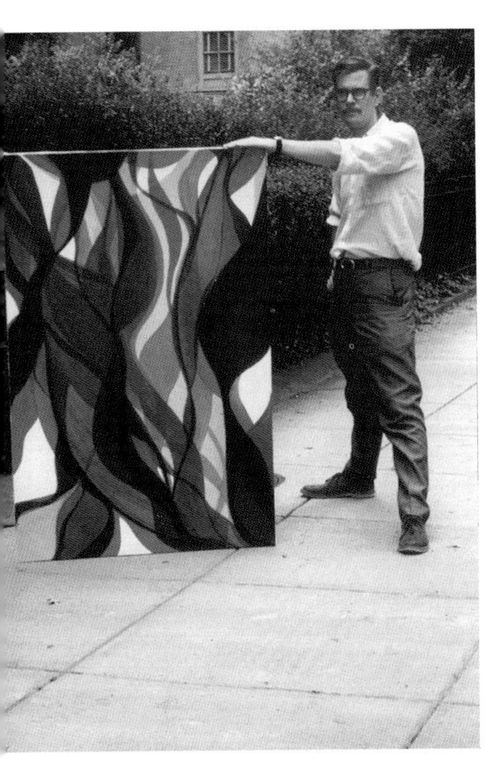

De Looper with one of his paintings from 1966

came in contact with Gene Davis (1920-1985). Other artists also associated with the "School," such as sculptor and painter Anne Truitt (b. 1921), report that Noland provided strong stimulation for Washington artists on returning from his frequent trips to New York. De Looper and Sam Gilliam (b. 1933), both still Washington-based at the time of this writing, are the stylistic and philosophical heirs of these pioneers.

In 1965 the Washington Gallery of Modern Art presented a pivotal exhibition titled Washington Color Painters *which included Louis, Noland, Davis, Downing, Mehring, and Reed. In selecting this title, curator Gerald Nordland was the first to attach the color designation to this group of artists who became the Washington Color School.*

In the 1950s and 1960s, The Phillips Gallery, (renamed The Phillips Collection in 1960) was a supportive and inspiring employer for many active Washington artists. In 1960 a wing was added to accommodate large contemporary works by key Abstract Expressionist painters such as de Kooning, Motherwell, and Rothko. When Duncan Phillips died in 1966 at the age of 80, his widow, Marjorie, and son, Laughlin, assumed direction of the museum which then consisted of a core permanent collection of 2,500 works acquired by The Phillips over a 50-year period.

Until the sixties, one of the few fine art dealers and perhaps the most important in Washington was Franz Bader, who ran the Whyte Gallery from 1939-1952, and in 1953 founded the gallery that has operated under his name ever since. The Henri Gallery has had a presence in the city since the sixties, and Jane Haslem, another dealer in contemporary art also began operating in Washington during the sixties. Barbara Fendrick opened a gallery under her name and Ramon Osuna opened Pyramid in 1970; both also specialized in contemporary art. Pyramid Gallery became Osuna Gallery in 1979. In 1964 The Washington Print Club was established to stimulate interest in graphic arts in the Washington area.

1966-1970

De Looper's first solo exhibition was in 1966 at the Jefferson Place Gallery, where he exhibited works described in reviews as "large blossom designs."[8] (Fig. 2)

Also in 1966, de Looper's work was included in the Washington Watercolor Society Exhibition, the Hope College (Holland, Michigan) Fine Arts Festival, the UNESCO and Brandeis University's Art Exhibit and Auction at the World Bank. Several of his paintings were selected for the State Department's Art in Embassies Program for the first time in 1966. In 1967, de Looper was selected for the second time for the Corcoran's biennial *Washington Area Show*. He was included in a list of only five "younger artists" praised for... *maintaining interest on successive visits to the exhibition.* His large *Blue Over Green* was judged as...*more fluid and relaxed, an improvement on his work [of] last season.*[9]

Jefferson Place presented solo exhibitions of de Looper's work almost every year beginning with his first in 1966 and running through 1974. The Washington Gallery of Modern Art's 1968 *Group Seven* show, organized by curator Renato Danese, included de Looper's work, and his work was also shown during this period outside Washington: in 1968 at

The Jefferson Place Gallery was organized in 1957 by Joe Summerford, William Calfee, and Robert F. Gates (all American University studio art faculty), and Mary Orwen. Alice Denney was the first manager. In 1961 Nesta Dorrance became the Director and the Gallery moved from Connecticut Avenue and Jefferson Place to 2144 P Street, NW. Throughout its twenty years of existence, Jefferson Place played a key role in Washington abstraction, exhibiting Davis, Louis, Noland, and others along with de Looper.

The Washington Area Exhibitions *at The Corcoran Gallery of Art were biennial reviews of the "best" of local artists, determined by open competition and a jury composed of luminaries from other cities, especially New York. "Purchase awards" were made of the works of top prize winners, which then became part of the Corcoran's permanent collection. By 1966 there was concern that many of the more successful local artists were not submitting work, and calls were issued for abandoning the jury approach in favor of Corcoran staff selection.*

Brandeis University in Massachusetts, in 1969 at Silvermine College in Connecticut, and in 1970 at both Pennsylvania State University and at the Baltimore Museum of Art's *Washington: Twenty Years*. In a review of the WGMA *Seven* show, de Looper's work was characterized by critic Benjamin Forgey as an…*almost complete disintegration of form so that the principal formal confinement available is the rectangular edge of the painting.*[10]

Dorothy and Sam Gilliam with Willem and Frauke on a trip to Europe in 1968.

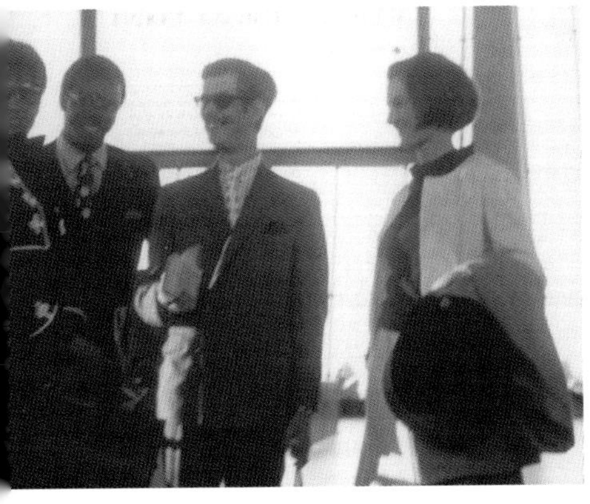

In 1968 de Looper and his future wife, Frauke Weber, joined Sam and Dorothy Gilliam on a trip to Europe which included a stop in London to see the Kenneth Noland exhibition at the Kasmin Gallery. The Gilliams went to Paris just before the student riots in June of 1968, and then on to Southern France, while Willem and Frauke traveled to the Netherlands and Germany to visit family.

In 1969 the couple was married and moved into the St. Regis building on California Street, in Northwest Washington, where de Looper had a relatively large studio space for the first time. He dates the beginning of his production of large canvases to this move. He continues to maintain his residence and studio at this Washington location today.

1971-1973

In 1971 Willem and Frauke, who was working at the German Embassy in Washington, drove a car across the United States. Up to that time, de Looper had avoided travel and had resisted rather than sought vacations. He preferred, as he has said: *my studio and the city; and during this trip I kept saying to Frauke: 'Let's just go back now!' I really wanted to get back to my work in the studio.* But, ironically, that trip was influential in many ways. It can be seen in his reference to

Many art trends during the 1970s continued to emphasize Minimalism, but a strong strain of artistic self-referentiality became apparent in the work of Robert Mangold and Brice Marden, among others. Conceptual art also gained prominence, as did "earthworks" and site-specific art, pattern and decoration, photo-realism, body and performance art, feminist art, and a range of other splits from the painting and sculptural modes which are often seen as the continuations of Modernism. By 1970 landscape and the color of the west, and to artifacts of Indian culture in subsequent paintings. A number of canvases have Indian names. Frauke was very influential, too, as she specialized in the cultures of North American Indians in graduate school. Since their first trip, the de Loopers have been to Taos several times, and also to Santa Fe to visit their friend and Washington gallery owner Manfred Baumgartner. He was responsible for introducing them to the cultural life around Santa Fe including the O'Keeffe museum at Abiquiu where they were among the first visitors when it opened. The de Loopers 'adopted' a young Navaho girl whom...*we have been assisting in small ways financially for about 10 years.*[11]

During December 1971 and January 1972 an exhibition of works by Washington artists personally selected by Marjorie Phillips was shown at The Phillips Collection. It included a de Looper canvas entitled *Chinoise*, which was acquired by The Phillips and then traded later that year for another work. As Mrs. Phillips noted in her signed remarks in the exhibition guide, the exhibition was of...*the museum's favorite artists...I had in mind a small exhibition to be shown in the Main Gallery, and it may be one of similar shows stretching into the future.*[12] In 1971 de Looper was also represented in shows sponsored by his own gallery (Jefferson Place), the Instituto Guatemalteco-Americano, the Northern Virginia Fine Arts Association, and the Art Society of the International Monetary Fund which were all in the Washington area. In addition, he exhibited at the Kingpitcher Gallery in Pittsburgh.

By 1972 the former museum guard had taken advantage of the many opportunities offered by what de Looper has termed

an important phase of American Abstraction was closing. Several of the prominent painters whose work had affected de Looper either directly or indirectly had died: Louis and Kline in 1962; Hoffman in 1966; Reinhardt in 1967; and Newman and Rothko in 1970. Both Guston and Still died in 1980.

In 1972 Marjorie and Laughlin Phillips hired Richard Friedman of the Metropolitan Museum in New York as the museum's first professional curator. Friedman left The Phillips Collection in 1975, and James McLaughlin who had been at the museum since the 1930s, became the head curator, a position held until his death in 1982.

the “formlessness of the place” (The Phillips Collection as an organization) to involve himself in many aspects of the museum’s work from bookkeeping, making and filing slides, clerical support, and arranging for photography for catalogues, as well as handling reproduction rights. In 1972 when Laughlin Phillips became Director of the museum upon his mother’s retirement, de Looper became Assistant Curator and, two years later, Associate Curator.

During the early seventies several of de Looper’s works including *Spring, Toujours, Stretto, Syrinx,* and two untitled canvases were moving from place to place as part of the State Department’s Art in Embassies Program. These works were exhibited in embassy residences in Canberra, Australia; Mogadishu, Somalia; Accra, Ghana; Port au Prince, Haiti; Santiago, Chile; Bucharest, Rumania; London, England; Managua, Nicaragua; Bern, Switzerland; Niamey, Nigeria; Peking, People’s Republic of China; and Asunción, Paraguay.[13]

In 1973 de Looper was one of 39 artists involved in the Washington Gallery of Art’s exhibition *Drawings and Small Works* which critic Paul Richard of *The Washington Post* characterized as demonstrating a *...new spirit of community growing in this city...which rules this exhibition but is apparent everywhere...*[14]

In a letter written in 1973, de Looper describes his prolific painting activity during this period: *I have a series of fairly large (8 x 10 feet wide) paintings which are new and [I] add to this supply with an average of one large painting per week.*[15]

Chronology of the artist

1974-1976

1974 was an important year in de Looper's career. He was included in the *Washington Invitational* sponsored by the Adams-Davidson Gallery and planned to coincide with the opening of the Hirshhorn Museum and Sculpture Garden. In the catalogue for the show, the director asserted that an... *atmosphere of freedom was palpable in Washington (and in the selections she made for the show), and that it developed as a direct result of the innovations of the Washington Color School of the 1950s.*[16]

Also in 1974 de Looper was involved, along with other artists, in exhibitions and performances that were part of *Art Now '74* at the Kennedy Center for the Performing Arts. For this event he designed *Sky Forms*, a work of circular and spiral forms of vari-colored smoke "painted" in the sky over the Kennedy Center building by a small skywriter plane. De Looper has noted that *Sky Forms* was his first and only venture into conceptual art.[17]

The Jefferson Place Gallery closed in 1974, and both Adams-Davidson and Max Protetch wanted to represent de Looper. He finally chose Protetch, known for his representation of minimalist artists. Before closing, Jefferson Place gave him a solo show, as did Protetch the following year. De Looper found the Protetch association *...very stimulating, since, at the time, Max was representing people from all over. Joel Shapiro, Sol LeWitt, Ed Ruscha, Vito Acconci, Pat Steir, and Ellsworth Kelly were in Max's stable then. I was heavily influenced by Kelly for a number of years, especially by his sculpture. During this period, I was the only Washington artist Max represented.*[18]

Historical context

The early seventies were years of expansion of the visual arts in Washington. The following government-sponsored museums were opened: The National Collection of Fine Arts (renamed the National Museum of American Art), the Renwick Gallery, the Hirshhorn Museum and Sculpture Garden, and the East Building of the National Gallery of Art. The Washington Project for the Arts debuted in 1976, under Alice Denney's direction, in an old store and theater at 1227 G Street, NW.

From May 29 to June 16, 1974, the Kennedy Center for the Performing Arts sponsored Art Now '74*, billed as "the first national arts festival," which highlighted "post object" and performance art, including developments in American contemporary painting, sculpture, photography, video, music, dance, and theater, with more than 50 artists participating. Highlighted in public relations pieces were artists Trisha Brown, Christo, Philip Glass, Robert Morris, Robert Rauschenberg, Richard Serra, and Stephen Shore. Four Washington artists were included (after a protest that none were on the original list): Gene Davis, Willem de Looper, Sam Gilliam, and Rockne Krebs.*

De Looper's father, Henri Bastiaan, and brother, Johan, at the The Golden Door *exhibition at the Hirshhorn in 1976. They are standing in front of de Loopers' painting which was included in that exhibition and in this retrospective (Cl. 17).*

De Looper also noted that in the latter seventies minimalism was "rubbing off" and that the "spareness" of works by Brice Marden and Robert Mangold, also represented by Protetch, became increasingly influential. During this period de Looper traveled frequently to New York on Phillips Collection business and made special efforts to keep up with the minimalist work of Agnes Martin and Robert Ryman.[19] He produced a few all-white paintings, exploring the minimalist vocabulary for a brief time.

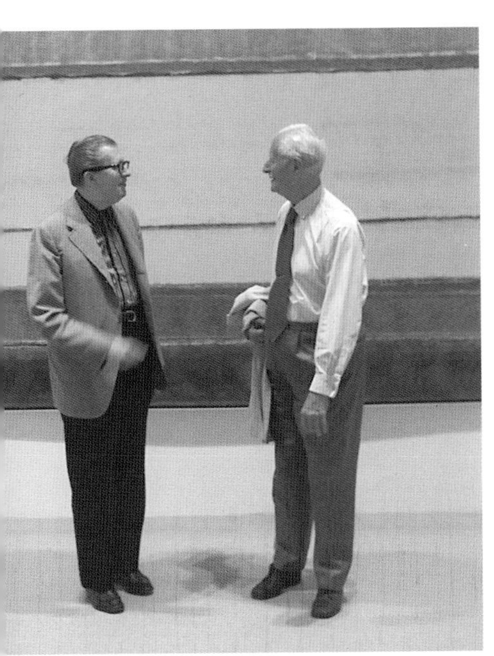

In 1975 and 1976 he was represented in two important museum exhibitions: one at The Phillips Collection, which featured his large canvases titled *Pasadena, Verde, Sur, Lamar,* and *Isleta,* and the *St. Regis Series* of ten small paintings on paper; and at the Hirshhorn Museum and Sculpture Garden's 1976 Bicentennial exhibition *The Golden Door: Artist Immigrants of America, 1876-1976*.

Also in 1975 Montgomery College, located just outside Washington in Takoma Park, Maryland, hosted a solo show for de Looper. The first retrospective of his work was organized at Northern Virginia Community College the same year. In 1976 the Federal Reserve Board, together with the National Academy of Sciences, sponsored de Looper's second retrospective with works from 1960 to 1976. The catalogue included an essay by David Schaff.[20]

1977-1978

In early 1977 concurrent exhibitions ran at Fraser's Stable Gallery and Max Protetch featuring large canvases and smaller works on paper. He was also represented by a 77" x 101" acrylic on canvas from 1975, donated by the Protetch Gallery, in

During the 1970s, the number of commercial galleries in Washington increased dramatically. Among those new dealers contributing to the active arts scene were

Hirshhorn's new acquisitions show, the first exhibition of purchased and donated art since the museum opened two and a half years earlier.[21]

De Looper's interest in printmaking dates to 1977. In a letter to Frank Gettings of the Hirshhorn, who had suggested that de Looper work with Tatyana Grosman of Universal Limited Art Editions in New York to create lithographs, the artist notes that his sketchbook acrylics, watercolors, and ink works *[which] I do quite a lot of...but don't usually show...closely resemble... prints that I might make, in that they are free and improvised in nature and very rapidly done...In the past, I have always thought in terms of originals, but with the encouragement of people such as yourself as well as (recently) Jacob Kainen and Alan Fern, I have begun to think in terms of making some prints. Obviously, I would have to learn from the ground up, since I know nothing about the process.*[22]

In June of 1977 de Looper was turned down for a National Endowment for the Arts Artist Fellowship, the first and only time he applied for such an award.

Also in 1977, at the urging of friends, Willem and Frauke joined a Smithsonian travel group for a Trans-Siberian Railroad trip across the Soviet Union. They traveled via Tokyo, (de Looper's first encounter with Japan), and also took a side trip to Samarkand and Taskent. This trip into the heart of the former Soviet Islamic republics was highly influential on subsequent work. As de Looper has said: *The blues and turquoises I began to use, and especially*

Manfred Baumgartner, Robert Brown, Nancy McIntosh Drysdale, Kathleen Ewing, Christopher Middendorf, Max Protetch, Jack Shainman, and Komie Wachie.

The ideas of abstraction were being carried into the area university art programs in small increments during the fifties and sixties, and then with more sustained impact in the seventies. Jack Tworkov had taught summers at American University from 1948 to 1951 before de Looper enrolled, Philip Guston was a visiting artist in the fifties, and Gene Davis was there for a brief time from 1968 to 1970. At the University of Maryland in College Park, abstraction gained hold in the early seventies and remains a strong focus of the department into the mid-nineties. Jacob Kainen, initially painting figuratively, and later becoming one of Washington's important abstract artists, taught at Maryland in 1969 and 1970; Sam Gilliam from 1982 to 1985; and Anne Truitt began teaching in 1975 and continues as Professor Emerita. Although de Looper was not formally involved in teaching, the environment in which he worked for so many years at The Phillips fostered the free exchange of ideas among the staff, most of whom were professional or student artists. In the course of day-to-day work at the museum they frequently discussed their own work and related aesthetic issues—teaching and learning of the best sort.

One of de Looper's photographs of the Islamic architecture from Taskent. The curved arches and bright colors he saw during this 1977 trip had a direct impact on his paintings.

the modification of my 'window' shapes were direct results of exposure to the color and complexity of the indigenous Islamic culture of Samarkand and Taskent.[23]

De Looper's small works on paper were first exhibited in 1978 at Montgomery College and at the Jean Marie Antone Gallery in Annapolis. Other exhibitions in 1978 were organized by Protetch, Catholic University, and the Chuck Levitan Gallery. The Chuck Levitan Gallery group exhibition of Washington artists' works on paper was de Looper's first exposure in New York. These important exhibitions of 1978 consisted of canvases which employed vertical rectangular shapes for the first time, and of new works on paper.

1979-1983

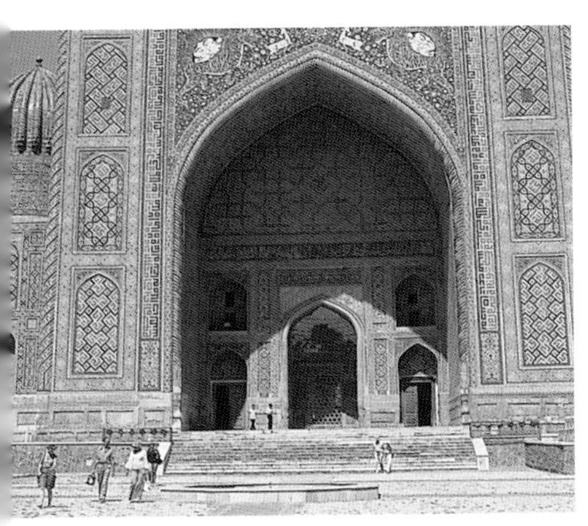

By 1979 de Looper was creating major exhibitions for The Phillips Collection such as *Franz Kline: The Color Abstractions,* and his painting career had become very well established. From 1979 to 1983, de Looper kept a comprehensive list of all paintings he made during these years, together with records of exhibitions and sales.[24] 1979 marked his first solo exhibition in New York, at the Sarah Y. Rentschler Gallery, and his second review in *ARTnews*.[25]

There were two exhibitions in Washington in 1980: a solo at the McIntosh/Drysdale Gallery, and another at the Corcoran Gallery of Art. Also in 1980, the artist made a trip to Florida where he placed four (and later that year, six more) paintings at the Medici-Berenson Gallery in Miami and three at the Hodgell-Hartigan Gallery in Sarasota. The de Loopers began annual visits to Florida in 1981 and continued these trips through 1994.

In 1979 the Max Protetch Gallery became Protetch-McIntosh. When Max Protetch moved his operations to New York in 1981, Nancy McIntosh Drysdale retained the Washington establishment and changed its name to McIntosh/Drysdale. In the nineties, the gallery changed its name again to Nancy Drysdale.

In the 1980s, several new galleries joined the Washington scene: Addison Ripley, Brody's, Jones Troyer Fitzpatrick, Marsha Mateyka, and Tartt. The National Museum of Women in the Arts and the new Smithsonian Museums, The Sackler Gallery and the National Museum of African Art, opened in 1987.

The 1980s witnessed an expansion of arts activities in the U.S. in many areas including the commercial marketplace, alternative spaces, and major museum exhibitions and construction. The decade may be most remembered for the flurry of Post-Modernist practice and theorizing, for

The de Loopers also traveled to Europe from mid-December 1981 through early January 1982, where the artist placed and sold work with two galleries in Hamburg: the Galerie L, which had hosted an exhibition in 1979 of paintings on paper, and the Kunstverein Springhornhof. Simultaneously in 1981-82, the Janus Gallery in Los Angeles held the first exhibition of de Looper's work (eight paintings on paper) in California.

At The Phillips, de Looper curated *Photographs by Joyce Tenneson* in 1980 and *Philip Guston: The Last Works* the following year. He also participated with Sasha Newman in curating *Arthur Dove and Duncan Phillips, Artist and Patron.* The beginning of the traveling exhibition, *Master Paintings of The Phillips*, dates to 1981-82 when it traveled to San Francisco, Dallas, Minneapolis, and Atlanta. This exhibition kept changing and expanding through 1987 as it moved out of the U.S., first to Japan, and later to England, Spain, and Germany.

In August of 1982 de Looper was appointed Curator of The Phillips Collection. He had served briefly as acting curator following the death of his predecessor, James McLaughlin, who had been Curator since 1974.

In this new position, de Looper accompanied the *Master Paintings of The Phillips* exhibition to Japan and then to Europe in 1983, representing The Phillips Collection at openings, and usually giving slide lectures as well. This phase of the *Master Paintings of The Phillips* was organized in cooperation with the Yomiuri Corporation, the largest newspaper company in Japan, to raise funds for the renovation of the original Phillips Collection building. The

Neo-Expressionist painting from Europe and the U.S., and for the ascendance of photography. However such painters as Richard Diebenkorn, Ellsworth Kelly, Brice Marden, Robert Mangold, Elizabeth Murray, and Frank Stella, and sculptors such as Scott Burton, Dan Flavin, James Turrel, and Jackie Winsor continued very vital work using an abstract vocabulary. In addition, painters like Susan Rothenberg and Anselm Kiefer defied categorization and reinforced the resilience of painting outside of trendy styles.

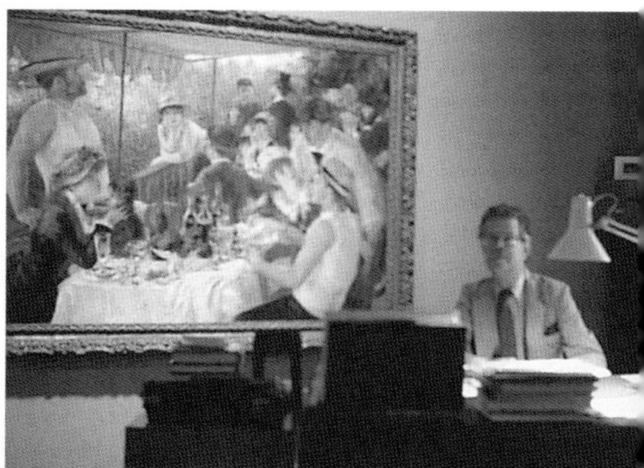

three-week stay in Japan included time in Tokyo and Nara, the two venues for the exhibition, as well as Kyoto and Nikko, and was highly influential for de Looper. He traces his use of metallic paints and foils and his diptych and triptych "screen" formats to this visit.

De Looper also traveled to Paris in 1983 to prepare the Bonnard: *The Late Paintings* exhibition with which the museum reopened after renovation. A major project for de Looper during this period was the first retrospective for Morris Graves. De Looper curated this exhibition in conjunction with Ray Kass. It opened at The Philllips in 1983, and then made a five-city national tour.

In addition to his numerous accomplishments as a museum professional, de Looper the artist was involved in significant activities during 1982 and '83. In 1982 the Wald Harkrader & Ross law firm presented a large exhibition of his work, and the Kornblatt Gallery organized a solo show for the artist and became his dealer in 1983.

1984-1990

De Looper at his desk at the Phillips. Renoir's The Boating Party *is behind him.*

From 1982, when de Looper assumed chief curatorial responsibilities at The Phillips, through 1987, he led the first effort to inventory the entire collection and publish a summary catalogue. Also during this period he and the staff organized several small exhibitions from the permanent collection which were successfully traveled to many regional museums for a fee, one of several strategies devised by de Looper to raise funds for the renovation of the original building. In addition, he organized *Kimura: Paintings and Works on Paper, 1968-1984* (1985)*; Three Washington Artists: Downing-Gouverneur-Gardener* (1985)*; Lyonel Feininger* (1985)*; Indian Art*

Today (1986); and *Leland Bell (1987)*. He also oversaw the development of *Outdoor Sculpture* at The Phillips Collection, a series of shows of individual sculptors' works: Christopher Gardener (1985); James Wolfe (1986); Peter Charles (1985/1986); John Van Alstine (1987); John McCarty (1989); Dorothy Dehner (1990); Steven Bickley (1990); John Ferguson (1990/1991); Jene Highstein (1991/1992); and Lisa Scheer (1992).

De Looper was in *The Washington Show* in 1985 organized by Clarie List at the Corcoran, and Kornblatt presented solo exhibitions of his work in 1985 and 1987. The latter exhibition, *Willem de Looper: Paintings from the Seventies*, featured works from 1973 through 1976. Ray Kass noted in an accompanying brochure essay: *The works of the late seventies embody a truly non-objective sense of content, as if they were windows in which there is no specific view...which infers a further level of abstraction [where] his subtle color achieves a heightened versatility, transcendently light-filled, or a veritable 'picture' of light.*[26] There were also solo exhibitions at the Tilghman Gallery in Boca Raton, Florida, in 1986 and 1988.

In 1987 de Looper resigned as Curator of The Phillips Collection but continued to work on several shows as Consulting Curator. His last exhibition as Curator was *John Graham: Artist and Avatar* on which he collaborated with Eleanor Green. De Looper worked on two 1988 exhibitions in conjunction with Linda Johnson: *Prints Washington*, and *Guillermo Roux*, and in 1989-90, on *Howard Ben Tre/William Willis*.

Sir Lawrence Gowing, British art historian and painter, was appointed chairman of The Phillips Curatorial Department at the time of de Looper's resignation. Gowing held this position from 1987 to 1989, retiring that year because of poor health. He died in 1991. Eliza Rathbone became chief curator in 1989. The Goh Annex at The Phillips opened in 1989 with de Looper's Howard Ben Tre/William Willis *exhibition.*

In 1988 there was a solo exhibition of recent de Looper work at the Shippee

Gallery in New York. That same year, the Smithsonian commissioned de Looper to create a print to be sold as a fund raiser for the Smithsonian Associates Program. The print was *Tunis I*, inspired by a trip Frauke took to visit friends in North Africa and by Dizzy Gillespie's jazz composition *Night in Tunisia.*

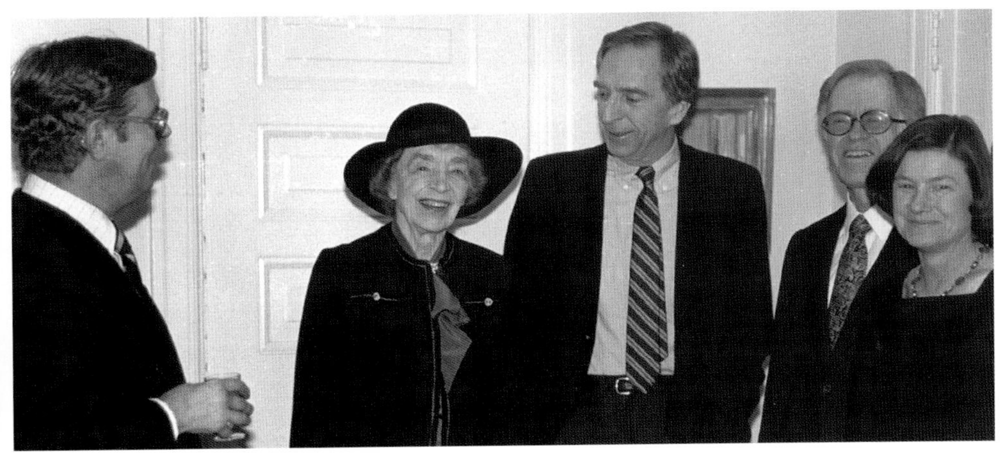

De Looper at The Phillips Collection with Marjorie and Laughlin Phillips and other members of the Phillips family.

*In 1989 the Jones Troyer Fitzpatrick Gallery (now the Troyer Fitzpatrick Lassman Gallery) in Washington exhibited small paintings on paper, which de Looper created initially as pages in sketchbooks that he conceived as single works which could ultimately be removed and framed individually. This show was presented in conjunction with an exhibition of recent large canvases at Kornblatt and was reviewed in *Artforum* by Howard Risatti.[27] When the Kornblatt Gallery closed in 1992, de Looper moved to Troyer Fitzpatrick Lassman.

In 1990 the Atrium Gallery in St. Louis, Missouri, held a solo exhibition of de Looper's works on canvas and on paper.

Terri Sultan came to the Corcoran Gallery in 1988 as Curator of Contemporary Art Charles Moffett, former senior curator of paintings at the National Gallery of Art, was chosen to succeed Laughlin Phillips in September 1991, becoming the first non-family member to direct the museum. Under his directorship the five large de Looper paintings in The Phillips Collection were exhibited in 1995 and 1996 in conjunction with a show of smaller de Looper works.

There have been other significant changes among the top curators of painting and twentieth century art in recent years in Washington: Jack Cowart left his position as Curator of Twentieth-Century Art at the National Gallery to become Deputy Director and Chief Curator at the Corcoran in the fall of 1992. Mark Rosenthal, the next Curator of Twentieth-Century Art at the National Gallery, left in 1996 but will oversee the Mark Rothko exhibition due to open there in the summer of 1998. Neal Benezra arrived at the Hirshhorn in January of 1992 as Chief Curator to fill the position vacated by Ned Rifkin. George Hemphill, previously associated for many years with the Middendorf Gallery, opened Hemphill Fine Arts in Georgetown in 1993 which quickly became recognized for its exhibitions of abstract painters as well as photographers. Many other names could have been mentioned in this very sketchy chronicle of individuals and institutions which presented important contemporary art in Washington. Even as this catalogue goes to press, other names will fade and new ones will emerge.

Although abstraction and color are clearly not the prominent forces in painting in the 1990s either in Washington or on the national and international art scenes, their unequivocal survival is important to note. As evidenced by the continuing vitality and fresh ideas in the work of Willem de Looper and other Washington artists, the history of this art movement in the capital city is not yet over.

1991-present

De Looper began making prints in 1991 with Smith Andersen Editions of Palo Alto, California, a printing studio and publisher that had worked with most well-known artists on the West Coast, such as Sam Francis and Richard Diebenkorn, as well as with Sam Gilliam from Washington. De Looper was introduced to the director of Smith Andersen by friends from Washing-ton who had moved to California. At Smith Andersen he worked on a series of monotypes printed on a large press.

The Troyer Fitzpatrick Lassman Gallery held solo exhibitions of de Looper's work in 1992, 1993, and 1995, and in 1996 concurrently with the retrospective at The Art Gallery at the University of Maryland in College Park. In 1992 and 1995 the Atrium Gallery in St. Louis also presented his work again in solo exhibitions.

In 1994 de Looper completed a suite of works in pulp painting and water-based monoprinting on paper during an artist residency at Pyramid Atlantic, in Riverdale, Maryland, a center for custom papermaking, printmaking, and the art of the book. He returned for two more residencies during 1995 and 1996. It was during the 1996 residency that two commemorative prints were produced in conjunction with the retrospective at The University of Maryland. De Looper's alma mater, American University, presented a solo exhibition of

De Looper in the studio at Smith Andersen in Palo Alto. On the wall behind him are some of the large monoprints he produced there in 1991.

De Looper enjoying the sun and broad vistas near Sante Fe. Black Mesa, which rises in the distance, inspired him and became the title of one of his 1992 paintings. (Fig. 15)

his work at their Watkins Gallery in 1994, and the Corcoran included one of his paintings in their *New Acquisitions* show in 1995.

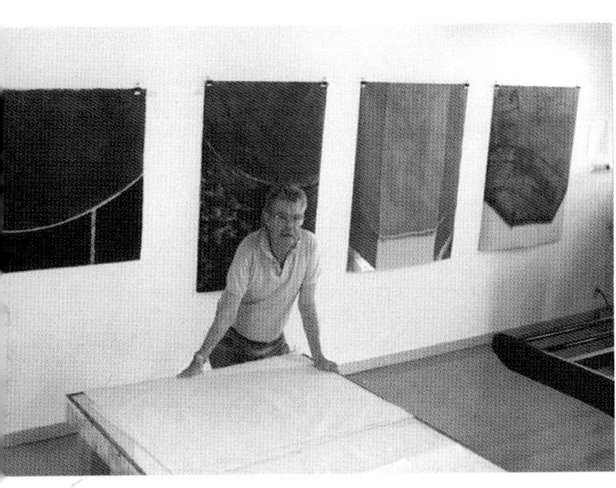

In late 1995 and early 1996, The Phillips Collection sponsored *Willem de Looper: Sketchbooks and Small Paintings on Paper.* This exhibition inaugurated the Museum's new series of single-gallery exhibitions devoted to contemporary art. In the museum's calendar publication, it was noted that: *Over the course of the last twenty years, [de Looper] has filled dozens of books with private and introspective works [which] are not preliminary studies…but finished paintings in themselves…he often turns the cover of the book into a painting…[and the small format] invites closer study of his subtle technique, strong use of color, and carefully balanced compositions.*[28]

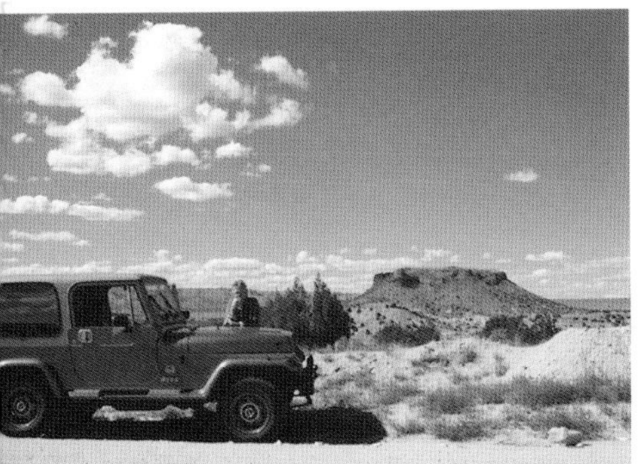

In 1995 and 1996, while planning for the thirty-year retrospective at the University of Maryland, de Looper organized his archives and did an inventory of the work he retains in his own collection. In addition he assisted researchers in the development of the exhibition and catalogue. Although Willem and Frauke traveled to Arizona to attend the high school graduation of their "adopted" daughter in June of 1996, most of the days, weeks, and months preceding the retrospective were spent in his studio producing new paintings for this and the concurrent exhibition at the Troyer Fitzpatrick Lassman Gallery.

[1] Interview with the artist by Mary Jo Aagerstoun, May 8, 1996.

[2] Ibid.

[3] Ibid.

[4] Ibid.

[5] Interview with the artist by David Schaff, *Art International*, 1977, Vol. XXI/6, December 1977, 46.

[6] Interview with the artist, May 8, 1996.

[7] Ray Kass, essay in exhibition flyer, BR Kornblatt Gallery, Washington, D.C.: "Willem de Looper: Paintings from the Seventies," October 24 to December 2, 1987.

[8] Pamela Howard, "A New Year–A New Look," *The Washington Daily News*, Friday, January 14, 1966, 25 (includes black and white photo of *Crimson Joy*).

[9] Photocopy of review of the exhibition by Andrew Hudson, *Artforum*, March 1968, 60-63, archives of the artist.

[10] Benjamin Forgey, "*The Question is ...To Paint, or Not...*" The Sunday *Star*, September 15, 1968, L3.

[11] Interview with the artist by Mary Jo Aagerstoun, April 22, 1996.

[12] Exhibition guide for *A Small Loan Exhibition of Washington Artists at The Phillips Collection*, December 4, 1971 to January 12, 1972.

[13] Registration-location-condition-receipt record copies, numbers 3869, 2058, and 2042; and letter from Willem de Looper to Mrs. Llewellyn Thompson, Director of the Art in Embassies Program, U.S. Department of State, September 16, 1976, archives of the artist.

[14] Paul Richard, *"The Community Art Spirit," The Washington Post*, Friday, March 2, 1973, B1.

[15] Letter from artist to Mrs. Speyer, July 17, 1973, archives of the artist.

[16] Dale Kline Birkel, "Introduction," *Washington Invitational* 1974 (Exhibition Catalogue). Washington, D.C.: Adams-Davidson Gallery, November 1 to December 7, 1974. Countering Birkel's claim that the artists included in the show were "followers" of the Color School, Benjamin Forgey of the *Washington Star-News* noted that "several of the artists were set in their ways before Louis and Noland developed their striking innovations in color," and that, instead, the show had "something of the atmosphere of an American University reunion. Three of the artists, Robert Gates, William Calfee, and Ben Summerford–were early stalwarts in the studio art department there and [are] still leading members of its faculty...[while] four others–Leon Berkowitz, Willem de Looper, Jennie Lea Knight, and William Woodward had at least some association with the department either as students or teachers...[This left] only two artists, Joseph Shannon, the independent realist and James Twitty, the flashy abstract painter who is largely self-taught [who] had no direct connections to this university..." the *Washington Star-News*, Friday, November 1, 1974, G1-2.

[17] De Looper noted ruefully that the piece was "even more of a conceptual piece, because the pilot didn't show up on the day he was supposed to and when he did, he couldn't do the colored smoke I had specified. But it was fun and gave me a new respect for artists like Christo, since there were so many logistics including getting permission from the Air Force to fly in that air space! But it was a good example of the kind of atmosphere among the artists at Protetch and a tribute to Max. There were lots of other Washington art movers and shakers involved with the Kennedy Center events including Walter Hopps, Jocelyn Kress, and Mary Swift." Interview with the artist, May 8, 1996.

[18] Interview with the artist, May 8, 1996.

[19] Ibid.

[20] In his artist's statement in this catalogue, de Looper states that "My ideal is to be an abstract painter, a non-objective painter, and even when the paintings contained figurative and biological shapes, my ideal was, as it is now, to have my paintings viewed in formal terms." Schaff, in his essay, notes that "De Looper has not heralded a radical approach to painting, in part because he works in too cosmopolitan a milieu, and because he has resisted fads and remained an individualist." From *Willem de Looper: A Retrospective*, 1976.

[21] Local press coverage of the exhibition praised "the intelligent gap-filling" evident in the acquisition of paintings by Stuart Davis, sculpture by David Smith, and works created since the museum opened in "the fields of abstract painting and sculpture (Jack Bush, Anthony Caro, Friedel Dzubas, Alan Shields, Willem de Looper, Gene Davis, Jacob Kainen, Joan Mitchell, Michael Todd...and Alma Thomas)." Benjamin Forgey, "Hirshhorn is Acquiring a New Look," *The Washington Star*, Sunday, April 3, 1977, G24.

[22] Letter from the artist to Frank Gettings, Curator of Prints and Drawings, Hirshhorn

De Looper in his studio with large and small paintings from 1981-1982.

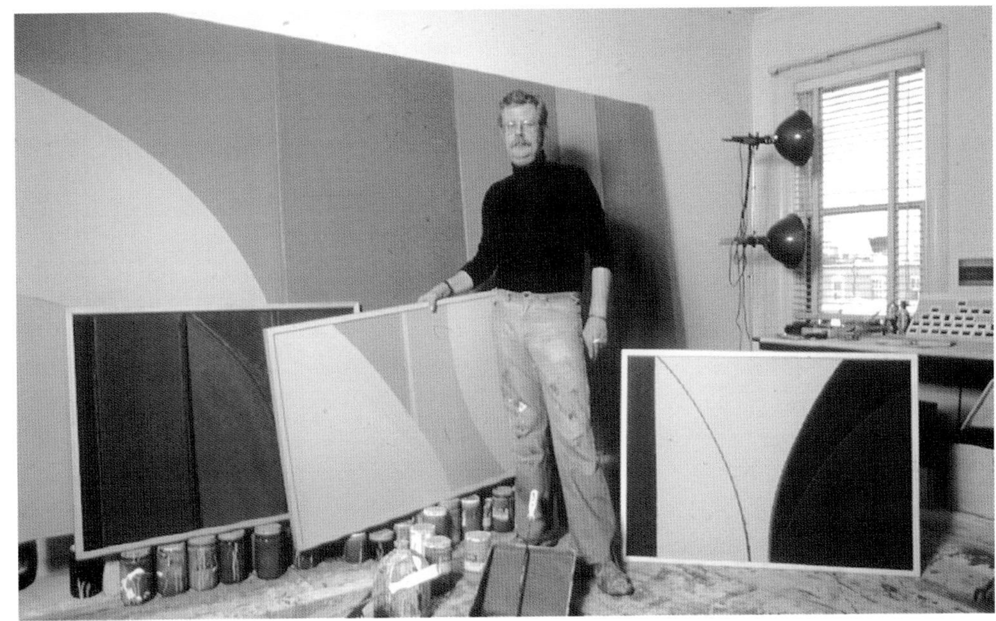

Museum and Sculpture Garden, January 27, 1977, archives of the artist. In a letter to Gettings, of April 12, 1977, Tatyana Grosman declines Gettings suggestion that de Looper work with her to produce lithographs because "Unfortunately my commitments are with artists with whom I have worked for so many years, and we are far behind with various projects." Letter in artist's archives.

[23] Interview with the artist, May 8, 1996.

[24] Book in the artist's archives; text on cover: "Record of Paintings - 1980-1981-1982-1983 de Looper." First entry dated December 1979, last one dated December 5, 1983. This was the first and only time the artist made such a record of his production. Interview with artist, April 24, 1996.

[25] Cynthia Saltzman, "Willem de Looper" (Sarah Y. Rentschler), *ARTnews*, December, 1979, 170. De Looper was reviewed earlier, in *ARTnews,* summer 1974.

[26] Ray Kass, "The Paintings of Willem de Looper, 1973-1976." from the BR Kornblatt Gallery exhibition brochure, *Willem de Looper: Paintings from the Seventies*, October 24, 1989 through December 2, 1990, archives of the artist.

[27] Howard Risatti, "Washington D.C.: Willem de Looper: Jones Troyer Fitzpatrick Gallery; BR Kornblatt Gallery," *Artforum*, summer 1989.

[28] Phillips Collection, *News and Events: January-February 1996*, 5.

[29] Because Nara was the Japanese capitol from 710-794, it has many Buddhist monuments. Today it still contains many of Japan's most significant cultural sites including the five-story pagoda and complex of buildings at Horyuji temple, supposedly the oldest wood structure in the world. It also has the largest bronze statue of Buddha in Asia (about 50 feet high) and a famous statue made in the dry lacquer technique imported into Japan from China.

[30] Michael Welzenbach, "Paint for Paint's Sake," *The Washington Post* (March 4, 1989), C2.

[31] Michael Welzenbach, "For de Looper, A Change of Color," *The Washington Post (January 11, 1992), G2.*

[32] Jean Lawlor Cohen, "Willem de Looper," *ARTnews* (summer 1992)*, 144-45.*

[33] Letter to Anna B. Frances (October 1995), archives of the artist.

Willem de Looper
Biography

ONE-PERSON EXHIBITIONS

Jefferson Place Gallery, Washington, DC
1966, 1967, 1968, 1970, 1972, 1974

Philomathaen Gallery,
University of Pennsylvania,
Philadelphia 1970

Montgomery College, Takoma Park, MD
1974, 1978, 1985

Max Protetch Gallery, Washington, DC
1975, 1976, 1977, 1978

Fraser's Stable Gallery,
Washington, DC 1977

Jean-Marie Antone Gallery,
Annapolis, MD 1978

The Catholic University of America,
Washington, DC 1978

Galerie L., Hamburg, West Germany 1979

Sarah Y. Rentschler Gallery,
New York, NY 1979

McIntosh/Drysdale Gallery,
Washington, DC 1980

Ward Harkrader and Ross law firm,
Washington, DC 1982

BR Kornblatt Gallery, Washington, DC
1983, 1985, 1987, 1989

Tilghman Gallery, Boca Raton, FL
1986, 1988

Shippee Gallery, New York, NY 1988

Troyer Fitzpatrick Lassman Gallery,
Washington, DC
1989, 1992, 1993, 1995

Atrium Gallery, St. Louis, MO
1990, 1992, 1995

Watkins Gallery, American University,
Washington, DC 1994

MUSEUM EXHIBITIONS

Corcoran Gallery of Art,
Washington, DC
Washington Area Exhibitions
1965, 1967, 1980
The Washington Show 1985

Washington Gallery of Modern Art,
Washington, DC *Group Seven* 1968

Baltimore Museum of Art, Baltimore, MD
Washington, Twenty Years 1970

The Phillips Collection,
Washington, DC 1975

Corcoran Gallery of Art,
Washington, DC 1976

Hirshhorn Museum and Sculpture Garden,
Washington, DC
The Golden Door: Artist Immigrants of America: 1876-1976 1976

The Phillips Collection, Washington, DC
Willem de Looper: Sketchbooks and Small Paintings on Paper 1995-96

RETROSPECTIVE EXHIBITIONS

Northern Virginia Community College,
Annandale, VA
Paintings from 1962-1975 1975
The Federal Reserve Board, jointly with
National Academy of Sciences,
Washington, DC
Paintings from 1960-1976 1976

The Art Gallery at the University of
Maryland, College Park, MD
Willem de Looper: A Retrospective Exhibition 1966-1996 1996

COMMISSIONS

Smithsonian Resident Associates,
Smithsonian Institution, Washington, DC
Serigraph Edition 150 1988

Smith Anderson Gallery, Palo Alto, CA
10 monotypes 1990

SELECTED GROUP EXHIBITIONS

Embassy of Netherlands,
Washington, DC 1956

Hope College, Holland, MI 1965

Washington Society of Artists,
Washington, DC 1965

Washington Watercolor Society,
Washington, DC 1966

Silvermine College, CT 1968

Brandeis University,
Waltham, MA 1968

Pennsylvania State University,
College Station, PA 1970

International Monetary Fund,
Washington, DC 1971

Northern Virginia Arts Association,
Alexandria, VA, *Local Color* 1971

Kingpitcher Gallery, Pittsburgh, PA 1971

Adams-Davidson Gallery, Washington, DC
Nine Artists 1974

Hirshhorn Museum and Sculpture Garden,
Washington, DC
New Acquisitions 1977

Fishbach Gallery, New York, NY 1978

Chuck Levitan Gallery, New York, NY 1978

Middendorf/Lane Gallery,
Washington, DC 1979

Janus Gallery, Los Angeles, CA 1981-82

Atrium Gallery, St. Louis, MO
Works on Paper 1993

871 Fine Arts, San Francisco, CA
The Book as Art 1993

Addison/Ripley Gallery, Washington, DC
Evolution of the Print 1994

Corcoran Gallery of Art, Washington, DC
Recent Acquisitions 1995

REVIEWS, ARTICLES, CITATIONS

Arts 1965

The Washington Star, Washington, DC
1966-1979

The Washington Post, Washington, DC
1966-1995

The Nation 1967

Artforum 1967, 1989

Art in America 1972, 1974, 1988

ARTnews 1974, 1992

Art International 1977 (6 color and 6
black/white reproductions)

New York News Journal, New York, NY
September 1979

Die Welt, Hamburg, West Germany 1979

The Washington Times, Washington, DC
1983, 1987, 1989, 1990, 1992

Interior Design July 1986

St. Louis Post-Dispatch, St. Louis, MO
1990, 1992, 1993

Riverfront Times, St. Louis, MO 1992

Washington City Paper, Washington, DC
May 1995

KOAN, Silver Spring, MD May 1995

Who's Who in American Art

Who's Who in America

SELECTED COLLECTIONS

National Gallery of Art, Washington, DC

Hirshhorn Museum and Sculpture Garden,
Washington, DC

Corcoran Gallery of Art, Washington, DC

The Phillips Collection, Washington, DC

The National Museum of American Art,
Washington, DC

IBM, Washington, DC
National Science Foundation,
Washington, DC

Department of Health and
Human Services, Washington, DC

The Washington Post Company,
Washington, DC

Riggs National Bank, Washington, DC

Federal National Mortgage Association,
Washington, DC

Pharmaceutical Manufacturer Association,
Washington, DC

US News and World Report
Executive Apartment, Washington, DC

The World Bank, Washington, DC

Westinghouse Company Collection,
Pittsburgh, PA

Bethlehem Steel Corporation,
Pittsburgh, PA

Phillip Morris Corporation, Richmond, VA

Goldman, Sachs, New York, NY

Citicorp, New York, NY

Federal Reserve Banks,
Miami, FL and Richmond, VA

Security Pacific National Bank,
Los Angeles, CA

Atlantic Richfield Corporation,
Los Angeles, CA

Rosenthal Automotive, Fairfax, VA

Owens Illinois, Toledo, OH

Victor Shargal and Associates,
New York, NY

Arnold and Porter, Washington, DC

Arent, Fox, Kintner, & Plotkin,
Washington, DC

Howery & Simon, Washington, DC

Covington & Burling, Washington, DC

Pepper, Hamilton, & Sheetz,
Washington, DC

Patten, Boggs, & Blow, Washington, DC

Rosansky & Kay, Washington, DC

Crowell & Moring, Washington, DC

Squire, Sanders, & Dempsey,
Washington, DC

Deloitte, Haskins, & Sells, Washington, DC

Witowsky, Weiner, McCaffrey,
Washington, DC

Lowenstein, Newman, Rels, & Axelrod,
Washington, DC

Cresap, McCormack, & Paget,
Washington, DC

Peat, Marwick, Main & Company,
Washington, DC

Washington Harbor, Washington, DC

Oliver T. Carr Company,
Washington, DC
Chicapee Manufacturing Company

Sterling Federal Bank, St. Louis, MO

United Savings, Rockwell, MD

Krey Distributing Company,
St. Peters, IL

Champion International, St. Louis, MO

Belvedere Inc., Belvedere, IL

Howard Hughes Medical Center,
Bethesda, MD

Willem de Looper
A Retrospective Exhibition
1966-1996

Checklist of exhibition

1 *Blodyn,* 1966
32" x 31"
acrylic on canvas
Courtesy of the
Watkins Collection
at the American University

2 *Untitled,* 1967
24" x 24"
acrylic on canvas
Collection of the artist

3 *Untitled,* 1967
48" x 66"
acrylic on canvas
Collection of Benjamin Forgey

4 *Summer,* 1968
61.5" x 49"
acrylic on canvas
Collection of the artist

5 *Red,* 1968
24.875" x 18"
acrylic on canvas
Collection of the artist

6 *Spring Sound*, 1969
20" x 20"
acrylic on canvas
Collection of the artist

7 *Syrinx,* 1971
84" x 75"
acrylic on canvas
Collection of the artist

8 *Untitled,* 1972
72" x 72"
acrylic on canvas
Collection of the artist

9 *Untitled,* 1973
87.5" x 96"
acrylic on canvas
Collection of the artist

10 *Untitled,* 1973
84" x 84"
acrylic on canvas
Collection of the artist

11 *Untitled,* 1973
72" x 96"
acrylic on canvas
Collection of Laughlin Phillips

12 *Untitled,*
Regis Series, 1974-1975
15" x 20"
acrylic on paper
Collection of the artist

13 *Untitled No. 3,*
Regis Series, 1974-1975
15" x 20"
acrylic on paper
Collection of the artist

14 *Untitled, No. 11,*
Regis Series, 1974-1975
15" x 20"
acrylic on paper
Collection of the artist

15 *Untitled*, 1975
48" x 48"
acrylic on canvas
Collection of
Mr. & Mrs. John Freidenrich

16 *Sur,* 1975
74" x 95"
acrylic on canvas
Courtesy of
The Phillips Collection

17 *Untitled*, 1975
77" x 101"
acrylic on canvas
Courtesy of the Hirshhorn
Museum and Sculpture Garden

18 *Untitled*, 1976
15" x 18"
acrylic on canvas
Collection of the artist

19 *Untitled*, 1976
15" x 18"
acrylic on canvas
Collection of the artist

20 *Untitled,* 1978
21.75" x 21.75"
acrylic on paper
Collection of the artist

21 *Untitled*, 1978
85" x 50"
acrylic on canvas
Collection of the artist

22 *Untitled (*Diptych*),* 1978
50" x 96"
acrylic on canvas
Collection of the artist

23 *Untitled,* 1979
72" x 60"
acrylic on canvas
Courtesy of the
Corcoran Gallery of Art

24 *II,* 1980
72" x 96"
acrylic on canvas
Collection of the artist

25 *Untitled,* 1980
72" x 50"
acrylic on canvas
Collection of the artist

26 *Untitled,* 1981
84" x 168"
acrylic on canvas
Collection of the artist

27 *Untitled,* 1982
30" x 39.75"
acrylic on board
Collection of the artist

28 *Untitled,* 1982
84" x 72"
acrylic on canvas
Collection of the artist

29 *Tunis,* 1983
78" x 100.25"
acrylic on canvas
Collection of the artist

30 *Untitled*, 1984
60" x 60"
acrylic on canvas
Collection of the artist

31 *Untitled,* 1985
78" x 100"
acrylic on canvas
Collection of the artist

32 *Untitled,* 1987
48" x 48"
acrylic on canvas
Collection of the artist

33 *Untitled,* 1987
78" x 100"
acrylic on canvas
Collection of the artist

34 *Untitled,* 1988
70" x 72"
acrylic on canvas
Collection of the artist

35 *Untitled,* 1988
60" x 48"
acrylic on board
Collection of the artist

36 *Untitled,* 1988
72" x 72"
acrylic on canvas
Collection of the artist

37 *Untitled* (Diptych), 1988
48" x 72"
acrylic on canvas
Collection of the artist

38 *Two Untitled Drawings*, 1988/1989
(Based on two larger paintings)
4.25" x 6.25", each
acrylic on paper
Collection of the artist

39 *The Duke,* 1989
80" x 60"
acrylic on canvas
Courtesy of
Atrium Gallery, St. Louis. MO

40 *Marked,* 1990
80" x 60"
acrylic on canvas
Courtesy of
Atrium Gallery, St. Louis, MO

41 *Native Colors #4,* 1991
24" x 20"
acrylic on canvas
Collection of the artist

42 *Native Colors,* 1991-1994
24" x 20"
acrylic on canvas
Collection of the artist

43 *Black Mesa,* 1992
48" x 72"
acrylic on canvas
Courtesy of
Atrium Gallery, St. Louis, MO

44. *Paso Doble,* 1993
60" x 60"
acrylic on canvas
Collection of the artist

45 *Untitled,* 1993
31" x 41"
pigmented pulp
Collection of the artist

46 *East West Encounter,* 1994
60" x 84"
acrylic on canvas
Private Collection

47 *Untitled,* 1995
48" x 48"
acrylic on masonite
Collection of the artist

48 *Untitled,* 1995
60" x 48"
acrylic on canvas
Collection of the artist

49 *Untitled,* 1996
18" x 18"
acrylic on canvas
Collection of the artist

50 *Untitled Artist's Sketchbook,* 1977
10" x 11" x .25"
acrylic and other media on paper
Collection of the artist

51 *Untitled Artist's Sketchbook, 1977*
11" x 9" x .25"
acrylic and other media on paper
Collection of the artist

52 *Untitled Artist's Sketchbook,* 1981-83
8.75" x 5.625" x 1"
acrylic and other media on paper
Collection of the artist

53 *Untitled Artist's Sketchbook,* 1982
8.75" x 5.25" x .875"
acrylic and other media on paper
Collection of the artist

54 *Untitled Artist's Sketchbook,* 1989
8.75" x 6.75" x .5"
acrylic and other media on paper
Collection of the artist

55 *Untitled Artist's Sketchbook,* 1994
10" x 10.75" x .875"
acrylic and other media on paper
Collection of the artist

56 *Untitled Artist's Sketchbook,* 1996
10.5" x 8.75" x 1"
acrylic and other media on paper
Collection of the artist

addenda:

In addition to the contributors listed,
the **RICHARD FLORSHEIM ART FUND**
has provided support for this catalogue.

All works from the artist's collection
are courtesy of the **TROYER FITZPATRICK LASSMAN GALLERY,**
Washington, DC

This exhibition and catalogue were made possible with support from:

The Glen Eagles Foundation

The Washington Post Company

The Henry S. and Anne Reich Family Foundation

Troyer Fitzpatrick Lassman Gallery

Laughlin Phillips

Jennifer J. Small

Philip Smith

Terry Gips and Ned Hitchcock

Nick and Carleen Keating

Minnie Klavans

Carolyn S. Meakem

Suzan O'Neill

Magenta C. Yglesias

Anonymous

Carolyn Alper

June M. Carlough

Johan de Looper

Kenneth and Kiyo Hitch

Linda Lichtenberg Kaplan

John A. MacLeod and Ann Klee

Sally Paynter

Stephen J. Lynton

James and Minna Nathanson

Lydia and William Preston

Janet Solinger

Jane Suydam

Nancy Drysdale

Alan and Lois Fern

Suzanne Silk

Mary H.D. Swift

Gordan and Betty Felton